I0816690

It's Never Too Late

It's Never Too Late

A MEMOIR

Marla Gibbs

with Malaika Adero

AMISTAD

An Imprint of HarperCollins*Publishers*

HarperCollins books may be purchased for educational, business, or sales promotional use. For information, please email the Special Markets Department at SPsales@harpercollins.com.

hc.com

FIRST EDITION

Designed by Jason Kayser

Library of Congress Cataloging-in-Publication Data has been applied for.

ISBN 978-0-06-335663-4

Printed in the United States of America

25 26 27 28 29 LBC 5 4 3 2 1

Contents

FOREWORD

by Regina King

To speak of Marla Gibbs is to speak of endurance, brilliance, and unwavering purpose. It is to honor a woman who didn't just defy the odds once but time and again, bringing her community with her every step of the way.

I first met Marla when I was a young girl cast in a community production of *Two Twenty Seven*, a play written by Christine Houston and staged at the Crossroads Theatre, which Marla herself funded and nurtured as a space for Black creatives. I wasn't cast as her daughter in the play. In fact, I played the fast-talking little girl on the block, but Marla, fresh off her massive success from *The Jeffersons*, made time to return to South Central and perform alongside us. That alone tells you who she is.

Later, when the play was being adapted for television with Norman Lear at the helm, Marla did something that changed my life: She fought for me to play Brenda Jenkins, her daughter on the show. She didn't have to, but she saw something in me. She knew we already had chemistry from the stage, and she pointed out to the powers that be, "Hal Williams and Regina actually look like they could be father and daughter." She put her weight behind me before the world knew my name. Thanks to her, I had the privilege of being her on-screen daughter and her real-life mentee for six unforgettable years.

What many people don't know is that *227* in its television form existed because of Marla's vision, tenacity, and integrity. She brought the project forward. She showed up every day with purpose, making sure our cast and crew were seen, supported, and respected. She fought for Black writers, makeup artists, hairstylists, wardrobe teams—people who looked like us and understood the stories we were telling. She was in the room with the writers and editors, shaping each episode.

Although she was given the responsibilities of an executive producer, she was never credited as one. The authority was hers in practice but not in name. Still, Marla never complained. She led with quiet determination, always centering the work. She insisted on a father being present in the household, on storylines that honored our dignity and humor, and on representation that would resonate through generations. At the time, I didn't fully grasp the depth of her advocacy—but I do now. And it continues to inform how I navigate every creative decision I make.

Marla is, without question, a spiritual warrior. She leads with faith, conviction, and a grounded, no-nonsense grace that makes everyone around her want to rise higher. They say a sword is useless in the hands of a coward. Marla has long wielded the sword of representation, equity, and opportunity. She lived these values long before they were hashtags.

She has always shown up for the invisible, for those who felt underestimated, like she once did. Her strength comes not from theory but from experience . . . lived, tested, and true. She is an alchemist, turning pain into power, struggle into story, and always landing the perfect joke at exactly the right moment.

Years later I had the honor of helping give Marla her long-overdue flowers: her Hollywood Walk of Fame star. Working with her daughter, Angela, and her grandson Amil to celebrate her was pure joy. Marla had broken barriers and lifted so many of us, and it was her moment to shine. I'm grateful to everyone who supported that effort. And as a special gift, my son, Ian, DJ'd her celebration. His joy, his music, his energy helped set the tone for that beautiful day. That's full-circle love. That's legacy.

Because our relationship began in a theater she created, one rooted in community and intention, this has always been more than professional. It's personal. Marla is family. And after all these years, we're still connected, still laughing, still showing up for each other, still shining.

And now, so is her story . . . right here, in your hands.

—rk

It's Never Too Late

CHAPTER ONE

Flowers While I'm Here

It's really something to receive your flowers while you're here, and from a group with such a legacy and integrity.

My work, for the last fifty years, has been about making people happy, acting out stories in theaters and on soundstages. I've won the hearts of fans all over the country and the world. I played roles on primetime network television, situation comedies that hit big in the 1970s and 1980s: *The Jeffersons* and *227*. These shows resonated with the masses—women and men of all ages—who my fellow actors kept laughing and also kept thinking and reflecting on serious issues in life. In effect, we raised the hip-hop generation who also emerged around fifty years ago. That generation raised young ones who also watched me and became new fans, finding my shows every day on streaming platforms and on the internet. Because of the love I continue to receive from audiences, I have remained relevant. Just in February 2025, I was honored with the Hollywood Legacy Award at the American Black Film Festival Honors. I stood onstage alongside seasoned and up-and-coming brilliant artists of today, including Giancarlo Esposito, Aaron Pierre, Keke Palmer, and Aunjanue Ellis-Taylor, at the SLS Hotel in Beverly Hills. The ABFF Honors celebrates Black artists who have made significant contributions to American entertainment and who champion diversity and inclusion. So, I was honored. It's really something to receive your flowers while you're here, and from a group with such a legacy and integrity. It's a bit surreal and beautiful and, let me tell you, sometimes a little overwhelming.

"Look, I'm still working," I said to the room full of industry movers and shakers as I accepted the award. "If you have some projects for me, my agents [at Momentum Talent] are standing right over there!" Well, my short acceptance speech went viral. Chile, a week later, I was on the set of *The Upshaws* television show! Mike Epps and I had worked together before. Wanda Sykes and Kim Fields, who also star in the show, are artists whom I love. The lesson is that you have to speak what you want into existence. And I'm living proof that if you're still breathin', honey, you can be achievin'. It is never too late.

I was also thrilled to be a cover girl in 2025. I graced the cover of *Essence* magazine, in the annual special issue that celebrates Black women in Hollywood. This was a full-circle moment. I was on the cover of *Essence* magazine nearly forty years ago, in October 1988. Then and now, it's awesome to be recognized as part of our phenomenal culture and history by such a beloved African American media institution. I'm truly grateful.

While I've had a public life and career in the performing arts for a long time, I was no kid when I started this journey. I was born and raised in the Midwest, coming of age in the forties and fifties. I was a wife, raising three children, with one on her way to college by the time I could say that I was a working actor. I dared to change my life in the mid-1960s. I migrated across the country to Los Angeles with my two sons and a daughter, not in pursuit of Hollywood but rather for a life less burdened by lack. I worked consistently and hard at all kinds of jobs—in the air travel industry, in hospitality at a hotel, and much more. But it was never enough. My marriage—to a childhood sweetheart—turned sour. As Nina Simone taught us in "You've Got To Learn," love was not being served at the table in our home, so I sought to establish a new home for our children. I succeeded in that. My children grew up to be extraordinary adults, artists and entrepreneurs who have made great achievements in life, including giving me some beautiful and loving grandchildren who keep my life full of love, inspiration, and excitement.

I believe in the power of storytelling and imagination, especially so when the stories mirror our actual realities. That's the secret sauce to a successful television show, play, or film. In playacting we exaggerate and, in the process, convey truth.

I was never a housemaid like Florence, but I lived among women who were, including women in my own family. I was a good neighbor, like Mary in *227*, not living in suburban Washington, DC, but rather in Detroit and Los Angeles, who tried to help, support, and befriend the people of my community.

I am a grandmother who cherishes her role. And in September 2024, a film I starred in was an homage to that. The short film, titled *Mildred 4 a Million*, stars me as a great-grandma doing everything she can to connect with her great-granddaughter. The story is sweet, funny, and poignant, as it mirrors the real lives of many elders, including me, who watch our younger family members get glued to their phones and miss personal connections. My character's efforts to gain a million followers are to gain the attention of her great-granddaughter, or her "GG," as she calls the great-grandchildren. Mildred succeeds, but by that time, her GG has already moved on to a new social platform. The film is hilarious and also deeply relatable.

I've played many characters in television, film, and onstage, and I'm here to tell you my nonfiction story of life offstage has informed all of my roles. I've had a rewarding and wonderful time having this career in make-believe. But nothing is more beautiful and rewarding than living with the ensemble cast that is my real-life family. They are the stars in the pages of this book. Our story is not always as funny as the ones that I've performed, though. Being a Hollywood success didn't exempt us from the trials of life. We've experienced pain and suffering, joy and laughter, setbacks and gains, togetherness and separation, just like everyone else in life. As Langston Hughes once wrote, we know what it's like to have "dreams deferred," and we also know what it's like to have dreams realized—in God's time and in ways we could've never imagined.

My *Mildred 4 a Million* character may have hit the lottery to win millions. But I'm here to tell you that, in my reality, I won for life. As the title of this book says, it's never too late for the blessings and the good things.

I was not raised by parents who were happily married to each other. They had two children together, like my ex-husband and I did. But, like us, they ultimately couldn't get along together. My parents, my sister, and I had all once lived with my paternal grandmother and aunt. But when relationships went sour, it was my mother who moved out of the house. She was outnumbered, and in the process, she left her children behind.

I did everything I could not to repeat generational patterns. I did everything I could to stay close to my children, emotionally and physically—at the risk of overdoing it at some point. Mothers sometimes hold on too tight. And sometimes not tight enough. I did my best and got some great results. I took my first acting classes as a way to bond more with my daughter in her teen years. Doing an activity we were both interested in—that was financially affordable—was just what we needed. It paid off for our relationship, our family, and my personal sense of well-being.

I was not raised by parents who lived happily ever after. My mother got pregnant with my eldest sister at the age of sixteen. Her father, my granddad, was a pastor, so of course he kicked her out of the house. My dad married her and brought her home to his mother and sister, whose relentless mistreatment of her pushed my mother away, and by the time I was two years old, my mother was gone. When the separation happened, their abuse of her then transferred to me. I grew up in a loveless home, and the choices I would make in my husband and friends would reflect my desperate need to be loved.

I have often made some of the best decisions of my life by thinking first of my children and following their lead. They are among the reasons that I've had a successful and continuing career in the performing arts. Now, more than a half century later, I'm continuing to grow in my career, and with the leadership of my grandson Amil, I have an online and social media presence. Aside from works of film and television I've appeared in, I've organically grown to having more than three hundred thousand followers. Being on social media keeps me in touch with my people—those who remember me for my early work and the younger ones who find me on the channels and platforms that make the sitcoms of the sixties, seventies, and eighties available to today's viewers. Like my breakout hit show's theme song, I'm still "Movin' On Up"! I may even reach a million followers one day like Mildred! That's a wonderful thing.

I've learned to cherish every day because they're always a gift.

When I received a star on the Walk of Fame in 2021, I was so overwhelmed by all the screaming fans (and the heat) that, chile, I nearly fainted. But if you were watching, you already knew that because it was televised. The paramedics came and asked the normal "Are you present?" questions, like "Who's the president?" "What day is it?" "Where are you?" When they asked me my age, I gave them my usual answer: "Thirty born in thirty-one; you do the math and don't tell me!" My daughter said she knew then I was good. I was able to go back out and finish the ceremony. It was a memorable day, and I could not be more grateful for my grandson Amil, daughter Angela, and TV daughter Regina King, as well as all those who donated to help make it happen. My star is right in front of Jimmy Kimmel's theater. He also donated and threw my after-party. Regina's son, Ian, was our DJ—what a beautiful, gifted, and sweet soul. We love you forever, Ian! So there I am, name engraved for everyone to walk by and see, right outside the building where *Jimmy Kimmel Live!* is filmed and near the Dolby Theatre where the Academy Awards is broadcast. Yes, I am there between Mahalia Jackson and Snoop Dogg, right where I belong. Between the godly and the street, cause I'm a spiritual gangsta!

If you were among the millions who watched the prime-time broadcast of the Seventy-Fifth Emmy Awards, you saw me once again self-promoting. Honey, I love to work. But first let's talk about my off-the-shoulder gown.

Like every other one of my fellow actors and Hollywood luminaries, I came to slay, as they say. I called my dear friend and designer Linda Stokes, with whom I have a long history. She's dressed a long list of stars, from the late singer Donna Summer and comedian Joan Rivers and the Supremes to Jennifer Lopez, Gwen Stefani, Janet Jackson, and male celebrities too, including the group OutKast, will.i.am, the Jacksons, and many more. My daughter was with me at the fitting and said the dress made me look "sleek, sexy, and vibrant." I said, "I'll take it." I wore a black velvet number. The sleeves I wore were long, although I kept one shoulder out for the drama. Everyone loved the look, and *People* magazine's headline read "*The Jeffersons* Star Marla Gibbs Wows on the Emmys Red Carpet at Age 92!" I appreciate their intention, but I'd like to point out that I'm claiming thirty, and that's that!

I've walked many stages, but it's been a long time since I received a standing ovation for doing so. Imagine that. I was delighted. Now let me get to the self-promotion part. I was there to present with the brilliant showrunner Quinta Brunson, whose *Abbott Elementary* has taken home several Emmys. Together we presented the gold trophy to Niecy Nash for Outstanding Supporting Actress in a Limited or Anthology Series or Movie. Quinta said that she was "overwhelmed to be presenting alongside someone whose career has 'literally spanned decades.'" Then she asked, "What's the secret to working so long?" and I said, "That's easy, baby; it's the wage gap. I'll need to work twenty more years before I can retire." Then I turned to speak to the audience and said, "If you great writers write something for me, I can keep working and cut into that wage gap. And Black don't crack, baby, and it's never too late!" It was a great night.

I made my first appearance at the Emmys in 1981. I was nominated for Outstanding Supporting Actress in a Comedy Series five years straight in a row, between 1981 and 1985. I have yet to receive one of the statues, though many believe I have more than earned one. With all the love, accolades, and awards I still receive, I agree. I do hold a belief in asking the

Universe for what I want and having faith that it will deliver, as God is all-providing. Two days after the Emmys, I was offered a role on my daughter's show *Not Dead Yet*!

I broke through ceilings and stereotypes playing a maid on one of the most celebrated shows in television history: *The Jeffersons*. I embodied Florence, the live-in housekeeper of Louise and George Jefferson, a couple who had done what few Black Americans could do in the mid-twentieth century. They built a business successful enough to purchase a big piece of the American pie: a luxury high-rise apartment in the sky. In real life, it was rare, and on television, it didn't yet exist.

A maid is the most stereotypical role ever reserved for Black women actors. But the Florence Johnston that I played let the character's personality, humanity, and sense of humor shine. She was not a prop or a foil for a white character or a male character to bounce jokes off of. She was not shy to display her wit and to exchange her sharp banter with her boss, or anyone else for that matter. The show was a hit, and so was I.

Florence Johnston is the gift that keeps on giving. I loved portraying her . . . and the way she behaved and even how she dressed in unexpected ways. She didn't wear a uniform; she wore the fashions of the times, including an Afro hairdo at some points.

The shirtdress I wore in character has since been installed as an exhibition at the National Museum of African American History and Culture.

The point is, I've been around a while, albeit under different names. I was once Margaret Gibbs, who touched down in Los Angeles, fresh from Detroit, in 1969. I did not come in pursuit of a Hollywood dream—though I would get it.

The people across the country—and the world—know me from my successful and groundbreaking television shows of the 1970s and 1980s *The Jeffersons* and *227*. These were situation comedies that took that category to another level. The shows were funny and entertaining and pushed the representations of Black people and women to higher levels in American performing art and culture. As a consequence, and without being preachy, my fellow cast members showed that television could give its audiences something better and greater than demeaning stereotypes.

Under the leadership of the now-late Norman Lear, Florence was not the self-effacing "yes, sir, boss" type of domestic servant. She was allowed to show her intelligence and self-respect. Her bosses were no Rhett Butler nor Miss Scarlett; they were a Black couple who, through their own determination and intelligence, lived the American dream of growing a successful business, nurtured a healthy family, and showed themselves to be perfectly imperfect humans who were laugh-out-loud funny without demeaning themselves or their audience. The show also highlighted interracial marriage, and the issues that were tackled were not forced but rather organic to the characters. The cast was led by the incomparable Isabel Sanford and Sherman Hemsley, and honey, they were the best comedic partners on set that anyone could ask for. We were an ensemble made up of veteran stage actors who had honed their talents in regional Black theater companies, including the legendary Negro Ensemble Company, established in 1967 and based in New York City.

By the time I landed the role of Florence, I was a single mother who had raised three children, my eldest being in her first year of college. I uprooted us all from the Midwest to Southern California in one of the most dramatic decades of American life, the 1960s.

It was a time of great Black leadership with the likes of Dr. King, Malcolm X, Medgar Evers, Shirley Chisholm, Rosa Parks, and Fannie Lou Hamer. We saw the loss of our country's leadership, including the Kennedys. It was a time of revolt, of "Black is Beautiful," and of the discourse on civil rights. It was a time of pride, and as artists, we embraced the responsibility of portraying characters that we could be proud of.

My sister Frieda was already earning a living as a background actor and gave me a landing pad on which I could rebuild my life, independent of my husband, Buddy.

I come from a line of women who sought love but never found it truly; however, the lack of it forced each of us to find ourselves capable of standing on our own two feet. We had to for our own survival, and in my case for the survival of my children.

Acting saved me at a time in my life when I was broken. The education and joy were a balm to my wounded soul. I had been a wife with three young children; now I was a single mother from a broken marriage. My daughter, being the oldest, inherited a lot of responsibility that took time away from her being a child and teenager. Because of that, she also grew up feeling unloved and discouraged from pursuing her own dreams and passions. She says acting saved her too. Perhaps this is why God had us start our acting adventure together.

As I practiced, the quality of my work grew and changed for the better, and so did my life. If a character had strength, I seemed to gain strength. I grew by connecting with the emotions of a character.

I was driven to pursue acting out of a passion to get out of myself and my current reality. That was my motivation. Artists do what we do because we love it. We do it because we have to. Through our work, we tell stories that demonstrate what people go through in life and how they respond.

You can have the love, determination, discipline, and motivation, but you also need good and knowledgeable people, devoted professionals, to work with you and on your behalf. In Hollywood and show business, you need agents and advocates.

My first agents were pioneer Black women agents Ernestine McClendon and Lillian Cumber. Lillian was my first agent and Ernestine the second. These women were not afraid to speak truth to the powers that be in Hollywood. They had to be that way because the Hollywood circle of agents overlooked and undervalued Black artists. The television-and-film industry functioned the same way that most every other industry in the country did, and it reserved only a small sliver of opportunity in what was a big, rich pie.

If there is a person who made the most positive difference in the way that I and other Black actors in the 1960s and '70s were received, it was Ernestine McClendon. She was the founder and owner of the first Black theatrical talent agency in New York City. She set up shop there and in Los Angeles. A former actress herself, she was a freckle-faced beauty, with enough fire within her to stand up and advocate for other artists. In 1960 Ernestine took out a full-page ad in *The Hollywood Reporter*, where she published an open letter to the film industry. She confronted industry leaders about the dismissive treatment they gave Black talent. She used a revolving door as a metaphor to make the point that her actors were ushered in and out of the rooms of opportunity without being allowed to stay.

This shook things up enough for me to land an audition for the role of Florence. It also taught me how to push further. I, for example, was the first woman (and Black person) to executive produce and star in her own television series: *227*. But I began speaking up for myself and my fellow actors long before that. On *The Jeffersons*, it came natural for me to speak up about lines, storylines, and even pay raises. There were both family and so-called friends in my life who tried to tell me I had no power and no talent. I quieted those naysayers, because as they say, "Success is the best revenge." But it's a revenge that also teaches. Because it allows those who try to thwart your dreams to see what is possible. I saw what was possible in my mother and father, who both beat the odds and became business owners, and therefore they laid the groundwork for me.

Sometimes we let our impatience win, and we end up self-sabotaging. We give up and accept less than what is meant for us. Sometimes we mute, or disregard, the messages that we are supposed to follow. I'd done that many times in my life, including my wedding day, when I knew not to get in that cab—I'll explain that later. The point is, when it was time to get on the plane and leave my past behind, I was following the messages . . . I was listening.

When I arrived in Los Angeles in 1969 from Detroit, Michigan, with my three children, I had a job in the reservations department of United Airlines. I continued to keep my "day job" with the airlines even after landing the role on *The Jeffersons*. The flight privileges were a godsend, particularly once Angela went east to attend Howard University.

I'm deeply grateful to United and to show business groundbreakers, including Norman Lear. His success is unparalleled because his shows tackled issues that revitalized our American culture and the arts. Were it not for him in the wider world of television and beyond, I wouldn't be famous. People know my name because of him. And he continued to share his light and platform with me up to his one hundredth year.

I'm blessed to continue to receive recognition and support. So many of my show business children have my back on the internet too. Snoop Dogg posted online that it was time for Marla Gibbs to have her "Betty White moment." That got noticed and shared by Jamie Foxx, rapper T.I., D. L. Hughley, Kerry Washington, Yvette Nicole Brown, and so many other influential artists of today. That kind of support reminds me that I've raised the hip-hop generation from its infancy.

In more recent years, I've made guest appearances on various television shows. On *Grey's Anatomy*, I played a woman with dementia, admitted to the same hospital where her granddaughter is a newly appointed member of the medical staff. The granddaughter is very upset that her grandmother mistakes her for her daughter who died, and it triggers her granddaughter's memory of her mother.

Jackée Harry, my friend and castmate from the series *227*, led the way for me to play the part of her character's mother on the long-running, popular daytime show *Days of Our Lives*. And I was a church archivist in an episode of *Un-Prisoned*, working with Kerry Washington and my longtime friend Delroy Lindo.

Best of all, my three children are beautiful, accomplished, and talented human beings whom I love and who give me reasons every day to be proud of them. My daughter Angela starred in a television series called *Not Dead Yet*. A brilliant actor, she's been performing, teaching, coaching, and working in film and theater as long as I have. Amil is her son and is an accomplished musician and composer. My third child, Dorian, is an artist too, who has worked on camera and behind the scenes as a writer and manager. And my son Jordan worked the sound boom on my shows for years before becoming a real estate broker. From the time I turned forty-four years old and became a prime-time television star, arts and culture have been a part of our family legacy. The industry made a good life for us. The practice of making art saved my life at a time when I wasn't so sure I was going to have a long one. We continue to heal and know that it's never too late to try.

My sisters and I were raised during the 1930s and 1940s, when the mindset about what was achievable for Black folks was quite different. My father would always tell me to "make sure you graduate from high school!" So that was the big deal back then. My mother didn't graduate high school, nor did any of my sisters, so when my father died, I made sure I finished school in honor of him. I thought that was going to be enough to get me started in life. That is when I discovered racism. I was a great student in high school and could get a job over the phone easily, but when I showed up, they would tell me the position was already filled or that they were not hiring Negroes. I realized my job opportunities were going to be limited because of the color of my skin. Growing up in a Black neighborhood, I had been insulated, and we had everything we needed. I didn't have to deal with racism. I felt Black people had power. I wanted to duplicate that in Leimert Park.

I've not only been a working artist for a long time; I've also built cultural institutions in an effort to preserve our culture through the arts. When I bought the Vision Theatre in Leimert Park, I dreamed of a place where Black people would feel their power and know their brilliance. I wanted other Black business owners and organizations to support my vision, but unfortunately some of them gave me a flat-out "NO" and offered no reason why. I heard a lot of things from people about what was said behind my back; one rumor was "she was supposed to come and ask permission to buy the building." Again, it's hearsay, so I'm not sure what the reasons were; all I know was I made my bed, so I had to lie in it. I lost the theater (and a lot of money) and left behind a dream. But God has timing, and now Shay Wafer, who actually started Crossroads Theatre with Angela, along with Tina Knowles, are taking over the Vision Theatre, and my dream will live through them.

I was also committed to doing television shows I felt were important to society. One show featured homeless advocate Ted Hayes, who introduced the dome housing concept for people living on the streets in Los Angeles. Ted was on *227*, and we also had actual homeless people as background. They were so excited to be there and did great jobs. I did an interview saying I would like to see the industry consider hiring some homeless people as background in films that required huge background scenes. The article received some complaints from background actors, because they said, "We're having a hard-enough time ourselves to get work." They didn't understand I wasn't talking about union actors, and these folks on the show were so good, I could see the light in their eyes . . . And to me, I was seeing hope.

Life spirals and brings you full-circle moments over and over in ways and in times you can't imagine. Like the labor strikes that put the TV and film industry on pause in 2023, just as the COVID-19 pandemic leading up to the strikes put the world on pause. There were strikes such as this when my career was just beginning in 1971.

The outcome in 2023 was a contract—achieved by the Alliance of Theatrical Stage Employees (IATSE) and the Alliance of Motion Picture and Television Producers

(AMPTP). One of the new requirements now is that there is more diversity in the makeup and hair departments for cast members of all races and ethnicities:

> 1. Each principal performer shall be given the opportunity to meaningfully consult regarding any hair and makeup needs so that production is prepared to work with the performer, including having appropriate hair and makeup products and equipment. If the producer is unable to provide qualified hair and/or makeup personnel to work with the performer, production shall reimburse the performer for the pre-approved cost of obtaining such services.

Now that's change . . . good change.

I am so blessed, and God and beautiful people are at the root of all my blessings. We have grown a garden of great work over the years, and they are the ones who continue to give me flowers. I want to name all those who have honored me, but I hesitate to list them here in fear that I'll forget one and therefore unintentionally slight the kind people who believe I've done things worthy of their acknowledgment. I'm deeply grateful to everyone and anyone who appreciates what I've done in my life and work.

I also want to recognize the flowers I receive from people

and organizations that aren't broadcast on national media, such as the Angela and John Witherspoon Family Foundation for the Arts.

The recognition I receive does not keep me from moving forward, because I don't stop living and appreciating my life and the people in it. An actor's job is to tell a story and give voice to a character. It's an important job because we need to tell our stories and to hear each other. We all go through things. We all have our challenges and our crosses to bear. I'm excited that the technology available to us allows us to have meaningful discussions with people all over the world. I want to create an online forum inviting people to share their stories of how they've endured tough times and overcome the odds against them.

I keep walking and looking forward. But as I do, I remember the steps I took with people who came before me and who came beside me—my mother, Ophelia Kemp; my father, Douglas Bradley; and my sister, the stunning Frieda Rentie. She is facing tough health challenges these days that are hard for me to witness. Frieda had no children of her own but thankfully was very careful with her money over the years, so she has the resources to pay for help.

She needs constant care, and while I'm not able to give her much help myself, Angela is an active presence in her life, making sure that her auntie stays in good spirits.

My children are the foundation and motivation for me

cultivating a strong family legacy and a career that makes a contribution to more than my singular but blessed life.

I believe that some of the experiences that cause us the most pain are also what can catapult us to our greatest joy, if we use them to become who we are meant to be. It is said that even wickedness can work for God, and you can see in several cases that the good and the bad were part of God's perfect plan. I'm grateful I finally grew the courage and faith to leave some things and people behind to forge ahead and create my destiny.

Roger Mosley, one of my early acting teachers, was cast as the lead in the 1973 blaxploitation movie *Sweet Jesus, Preacherman*. Roger asked the casting director to see me, and I ended up with the role of Beverly Solomon, a church member, in the story of a gangster posing as a Baptist preacher to accomplish his dirty deeds. It was my first film. I learned to visualize my goals and aspirations. So, where a career in television was concerned, I began to visualize and say, "I want to do that show, thank you." I thanked the Universe ahead of time. Sure enough, I landed roles on primetime shows like *Cold Case*, *ER*, and others.

My birth year says I'm thirty three times over, but I choose to vibrate on thirty. We are spiritual beings as well as physical, and as such, we are ageless and timeless. My choosing to stay at thirty years old has nothing to do with looks and trying to act like I'm thirty. It has everything to do with the spirit of thirty. I've learned not to worry about age and simply think about what I want to do with my life and know that I can still do it. No matter what age I am, if I want to accomplish something, I'm going to give it a try—and since I'm thirty, I'm expecting to do it.

Margaret Bradley Gibbs never imagined in 1969, when she landed in Los Angeles with the intention of jump-starting a new life, that it would include becoming a household name and a television star called Marla.

I truly believe everything we do and everyone we meet are put in our path for a purpose. There are no accidents; we're all teachers and students. I do believe if we can conceive of something and believe it, we can achieve it. It's called faith! Faith and trust in the Divine. We have to pay attention to the lessons we learn, trust our positive instincts, and not be afraid to take risks or not wait for some miracle to come knocking at our door.

CHAPTER TWO

A Mother's Intuition

Love is not just an emotion. . . .
Love is a verb! A verb that includes
quality time, respect, patience,
understanding, and communication.

My mother, Ophelia Kemp, was a force to be reckoned with. She was a young, pretty girl when my father spotted and claimed her. Out of necessity and choice, she grew into a formidable woman who didn't let the tenor of the times stop her from carving out a life on her own terms. She sought to be a faithful follower in the church led by Detroit's legendary Prophet Jones. But she would eventually establish her own church and garner a following of believers who respected and recognized her gifts as faith based. She was a business leader and a clairvoyant. People would stand in line for hours to get a spiritual reading from her.

I didn't appreciate her lesson and example as much as others did. I had some things to go through. My young life was defined by circumstances and people who came into my life to set me back and knock me down, sometimes literally, before I could get on my feet for any length of time.

My father had already been married and divorced when he started going up to Racine, Wisconsin, where he met my mom. He went there with his friends to party and enjoy his single life. That's where Douglas Bradley met Ophelia Kemp. She lived in that town and would sneak out of the house with her sister Vera to go to the same parties. She was light-skinned, or, as they said back then, a redbone, with a face full of freckles and the prettiest legs. She also was full of personality.

Ophelia was a preacher's kid. Her father was furious and kicked her out of the house when he learned of her pregnancy. He found it unacceptable for a daughter of his and thought she would contaminate her younger sister Vera. Their mother had passed at a young age, when Ophelia was four years old. So when her dad turned his back on her, Douglas was all she had.

He decided to marry my mom. He was living with his mother Hattie and his aunt Bell. They were less than pleased to meet his pregnant sixteen-year-old wife, much less invite her into the family. They treated her as if she were common. Maybe they were also a bit jealous of her youthful exuberance.

The sisters may have disliked this pretty young thing, but they managed to fall in love with the baby she would deliver and name after her own sister—a child named Vera Louise. Two years later, I was born to Douglas Bradley and Ophelia Kemp and named Margaret. Frieda came two and a half years after me. One of the earliest stories about me that I can recall is about how a man passed by my mom holding me—a fat, little babe in her arms—on a Chicago sidewalk and said, "You should call her Dimples." That's how I got my nickname. Louise, my older sister, was called Dootie, and my youngest sister, Frieda, was called Peaches.

My father's mother and sister treated me differently from my older sister because they didn't believe I was my father's child. They convinced themselves that my mother was fooling around. Mother got a job working at a grocery store. She wanted to contribute to the family and would do so by bringing extra cans of food home for all of us. Instead of being grateful, my grandmother assumed the worst about how Mother was able to bring home groceries and accused my mother of having an affair with her boss. Ophelia was industrious, maybe a little slick, but not fast, as people called loose women back then. She would dent cans of food knowing the store could not sell them, then ask if she could bring them home to her family. The store owner allowed her.

My grandmother and aunt convinced my father that I was Mother's boss's child. They kept the story going and ultimately won his agreement to take my mother to court to prove she was an adulterer. They were proven wrong in court. My mother won on principle, but the damage to her Spirit and our family had already been done. The trust between my mother and father was broken and never to be mended. When my father didn't stop his mother from taking my mother to court, her heart was broken.

Mother was driven out of our family household when I was two years old, leaving Louise and me in the home with our dad, his mother, and his aunt. Daddy was loving to me and even called me by another nickname: Princess Margaret. I don't know why my father's people doubted that I was his. I looked just like him, down to the knock-knees and pigeon toes.

Grandma Hattie seemed to get joy making a difference between Vera Louise and me. She'd sneak and give Louise candy, but when I asked for some, she'd lie and say it was gone. Now, you have to understand that I was the type of child who asked for candy, because I already knew she had it, and I knew where it was. I'd ask, "Can I have some candy?" Grandmother would say, "I don't have any more." Then I'd say, "Yes, you do. It's right on top of the china cabinet in the dining room." Instead of candy, I'd get a whooping for my smart mouth. She was just icy to me.

I missed having the kind of grandmother everyone talks about. The warm one to whom you can do no wrong. I would go to hug her, and she would push me away. I can't tell you how much that hurt. Even a happy memory of my father standing up for me is tinged with hurt. I overheard him say to Grandma Hattie about me, "You already drove her mother away . . . just stop picking on her!" That day I felt good. Like I had a protector.

When I was young, I often felt I was a mistake. I didn't belong in that family, and I didn't belong in the world. I would do crazy things like hold my breath, hoping I could stop myself from breathing. I'd finally have to give in and take a breath, and this would upset me. I just wanted to disappear.

The house we lived in used to belong to a Mafia crime boss named Big Jim Colosimo, nicknamed Diamond Jimmy. Colosimo immigrated to the US from southern Italy and founded the crime syndicate in 1895. He got rich from what were ultimately hundreds of whorehouses in Chicago. He expanded his business into gambling and racketeering. He drew the line at bootlegging. His stubbornness cost him his life. He was shot in the head in 1920. And that's when the Colosimo Family became known as the Chicago Outfit. They fought off other gangs, including one called Black Hand, to essentially control business on the South Side of Chicago, where we and masses of other Black people lived in the 1920s.

When I was eleven years old, I made a habit of sneaking out of the house in the middle of the night and walking three miles to the beach alone. As dangerous as that sounds, it gets worse. When I got to the freeway, I'd dodge the cars and run across to the other side. I was young, so I didn't understand I was suicidal. I remember one day a driver had to slam on their brakes to keep from hitting me. When I saw the panic in the driver's eyes, I realized I could have hurt them too. So I stopped that.

Once I made it across the expressway to the beach, I'd sit on the big rocks and look out at the water. I couldn't swim and was way too chicken to jump in. Imagine that. I was crazy enough to dodge cars on an expressway, but drowning involved being in water, and I wasn't about to do that.

It wasn't always bad in my house. I do have some good memories. My aunt Bell would feel bad for me sometimes and do something sweet. I remember once, when I was fourteen and sick with a cold, Aunt Bell took me to Thirty-First Street, to a little shop where we took pictures together. I had on my red sloppy-joe sweater that my mother sent me, so it was really special and a lot of fun. Anytime Mother sent something red, it was for me, and if it was blue, it was for Louise. I still have that picture of Aunt Bell and me. It was such a good day, until we got back to the house. Once inside, Aunt Bell reverted back to being mean. I learned later that a belief system around love had been created from these early years. I was taught that love hurts, that you can't trust kindness, and even worse, that I wasn't worthy of either.

You know, there are always days that stand out in our lives, no matter how old you get. One of my most vivid experiences of childhood was my first day of kindergarten. My mother surprised me and came to town to walk me to school. I was ecstatic. Mother was beautiful and had such a charismatic personality; you wanted to be around her all the time. I thought we were finally going to spend time together. But once we got to the classroom, Mother told me she was going back to Detroit. Why couldn't she stay for the day? I started crying. I had so much to tell her. The crying got worse. When she left, I couldn't stop crying. The teacher didn't know what to do with me, so she locked me in the bathroom. I had sliced my thumb trying to cut potatoes at home, and when I pulled on the door to get out of the bathroom, it made the cut open up. I was bleeding all over everything. When the teacher finally checked on me, she saw the blood, and she felt bad. She said, "Come on, honey, you're going to help me water the plants and flowers today, okay?"

Walking around watering the plants cheered me up and kept me busy. By the time school was out and I arrived back at home, Mother was long gone.

I would get to see my mother maybe once a year. She would spend a couple of days with me and Vera and then go back. I remember she wore a perfume called Toujours Moi by Corday. My sister and I always went to South Park Avenue to wait for the taxi she'd arrive in. As she got out, we'd look down, see her beautiful legs, and say, "There she is!"

There were so many questions I had, but she didn't have the time to answer them all. When I was older, I wanted to know about boys and how to tell if they liked me. I wanted to tell her how my grandmother was treating me, how some of the girls were treating me, but mostly I wanted to talk her into coming back. But I never got to do that.

In the small window of time she was in Chicago, my mother tried to impart some of her wisdom, but it wasn't ever enough. Sadly most of it was lost.

When I was grown, my mother and I spent more time together, and I learned her story. She told me that when she was still living with us, she would complain about my father not working, and Grandma Hattie would tell her, "My son doesn't have to work." Meanwhile, my mother was holding down a job . . . the very job they harassed her about. When she got tired of their mistreatment and left, Hattie later found her and begged her to return. She said my father was losing his mind.

Hattie promised Mother, "If you come back, I won't even come into your room. I won't interfere in any way." But it was too little, too late. My mother said, "No. You were his mother, and I understand that, but I was his wife, and he was supposed to look out for me. He was supposed to protect me, and he didn't." My father never got over losing my mother.

After she left, he started working very hard and ended up owning two businesses. In fact, he worked himself to death. My dad was smart and full of business savvy. He read a book and learned how to fix cars, eventually opening a car repair business. Brad's Garage employed three or four mechanics and was successful. He also started an ice business and bought three ice trucks, later expanding it to five. He would deliver twenty-five, fifty, and a hundred pounds of blocks of ice, sometimes carrying them on his back up two or three flights of stairs. This was during a time when we had iceboxes instead of refrigerators. I suppose that's what caused his hernia. I think my father thought that if my mother saw how hard he was willing to work, she'd come back, but she never did.

When my mother first left, she only moved around the corner from us on South Park so she could be close. As time moved on, she began dating. Dad was probably spying on her, because he found out she had a boyfriend. He went over to Mom's house, and when he saw her boyfriend, Dad beat him so badly, he caused the man to lose his eye. Mom knew she was going to have to move farther away if she was going to have a life.

Ophelia Kemp was now on her own and was trying to get settled so she could take Louise and me with her. After she left my father, she wound up pregnant again and had my sister Frieda. I think Mom was so young, she thought she needed someone to take care of her, especially now with three children. She met a man named Chester Rentie. He was known as the mayor of Paradise Valley in Detroit, Michigan. Chester was a booking agent for talent, and he once managed jazz vocalist Betty Carter. He told my mother she could do better if she moved to Detroit. Mom needed a new start and agreed to move to Detroit, where Chester helped her get a nice house. She took Frieda with her, and we hoped we were next.

Chester and Mother dated for years; it was a good relationship—at least to her. My experience was quite different. Chester could not be trusted. My mother told him when he was in Chicago to go check on me. I didn't understand the feeling I had, but I knew I was uncomfortable around him. When he got to our house in Chicago, I stayed in the yard with my dog, because I knew he wouldn't come out there. My grandmother said, "Mr. Rentie is leaving. Come and say goodbye." I yelled through the door, "BYE!" I waited awhile, and when I felt sure he was gone, I went inside and up to the bathroom. To my dismay, Chester was waiting for me there. When he saw me, he grabbed me and held my face and then forced his tongue in my mouth. I had no idea what was happening. I thought he had turned his lips inside out. It was wet and slimy, and it made me throw up. I don't know if he ever touched my other sisters; we never talked about it. I know that he and Mother took Frieda everywhere, and for years people thought Frieda was his child because Mother gave Frieda his last name. I didn't tell my mother what happened with Chester kissing me until years later, but I was relieved when she caught him cheating, because that ended their relationship.

In order to get work and make moves, my mother hid the fact that she had two daughters back in Chicago. It just didn't look good for an unmarried woman to have three kids. So she told Frieda to also say she was an only child. One summer when we were visiting Mother, Louise went across the street to visit Frieda's friend. When her mother asked Louise who she was, she replied, "I'm Frieda's sister." The mother said, "No, you're not. Frieda is an only child." This really hurt Louise, and she took it out on Frieda. She picked on her all the time and could be very mean. I was Frieda's big sister, so I tried to stop Louise when I could. Mother told Louise that Frieda was following her orders and was told to lie, but Louise didn't care.

I think Louise was jealous because Frieda was pretty. She looked like a little doll baby. To add insult to injury for Louise, Frieda had Ophelia, and we felt like we didn't. I, on the other hand, was more focused on my dad. I always wanted my mother and father to get back together, and I knew my father wanted that too.

When my grandma Hattie sent me to Detroit for a visit, I decided I'd convince my mother to return to my father while

I was there. Before I left, I told him, "I'm going to bring her back." When I got there, I rang the bell, and a man opened the door. I was reluctant to go in, but then my mother appeared behind him and said, "Come on in, baby. This is your father," which was absolutely the wrong thing to say to me.

The man at the door was Charles Cady, and my mother had married him. I wanted to turn around then and there and go back to Chicago. That whole visit, I stayed in my room as much as possible. They tried to get me to go horseback riding and to other places, but I always used homework as an excuse. Frieda would go with them, but I would stay home.

After Mother and Chester broke up, she began to come into her own. I think she started to realize that she was smart and talented. She sang soprano on a radio show and became an entrepreneur, which was extremely rare for Black women at that time. Mother also owned a haberdashery and a lingerie store, and later opened a restaurant—that's where she met Charles Cady.

Mother and Charles started an illegal numbers business and became very successful. My mother decided that since they had a nice house and money, she would blend their children together. Louise and I moved in, and Charles's daughter, Susie, joined us and became my fourth sister. She had a brother named Donald, but he didn't come. We were all about the same age, and Susie fit right in.

Mother sent us to Northern High in Detroit. This was

the first school I'd ever gone to that was interracial. I really liked it, and the kids were nice.

While I was living with my mother and attending Northern High School in Detroit, I got recruited by the vice principal to make an appearance as an actor on a TV show called *Juvenile Court*. I ran into him at a grocery, where he was moonlighting as a product demonstrator. He asked if I wanted to try my hand at it. I did the sales demonstration, and when I was done, he looked at me and said, "You're pretty good." Turns out he was an actor in the Screen Actors Guild. He told me about *Juvenile Court* and arranged for me to be on the show and sent me a script.

The script had a lot of dialogue, but I'm a fast study, so I learned it all pretty quickly. When I got there, I was disappointed, though, because they didn't use any of the script. They had given it to me as a reference, so I'd understand what was going on, and when the judge asked me questions, I could answer them. I didn't know it then, but they wanted me to improvise the scene. The case was about a woman whose little boy injured a passenger when he threw a rock at a train and broke a window. The authorities wanted to put him in juvenile hall. In my role, I was fighting for him to stay out. I was telling them he was a young kid with no place to play, that we lived above a liquor store and he didn't have a father. When my mother and Aunt Vera saw it, they said, "You were really good, and we believed you." So that was my first acting job that aired on TV. Even though I enjoyed doing the role, I still didn't think of acting as a possible career. There were signs that acting was in my soul, though; I just didn't recognize it until much later. Whenever I went to the movies, I would internalize the characters without fail. I was a sensitive soul, and my friends would all look at me to see if I was crying during an emotional scene. There was a film called *The Biscuit Eater* that came out in 1940. Biscuit was a dog who ended up being shot for stealing chickens. I cried so hard in the theater, you would have thought it was my dog. I believed that world and the actors. Sometimes I would get so wrapped up in a character that, after seeing a movie, it was hard to let it go.

I remember I went to see Joan Crawford in *Possessed* in 1947. When the movie ended, I couldn't get on the bus to go home. It was as if I had become her character, and her experiences were now mine. I had to just walk and walk for a while to release the emotions and reset myself. Even to this day, if I watch something—say, *Days of Our Lives*—then later, in the middle of the night, I'm still trying to solve the problem. I have to tell myself to stop and go to sleep. I've always been like that. Some of my friends have teased me about it, called it silly, but hey, it's who I am.

I also loved musicals. I mean . . . LOVED them! I used to sing around the house when others weren't there, but I never saw that as a gift. Plus, I thought my sister Louise had a better voice. We would sing while in the Catholic boarding school during service, and her voice would just rise above the others so nicely. Louise was good but never tried her hand at singing. I, on the other hand, was singing all the time.

My grandmother and Aunt Bell surprised me and bought me a dress to go compete in an amateur night competition. They both came to the competition at the Terrace Theater, and so did my father! They supported me two or three times, but unfortunately I never won when they were there. Then one time I went with only my friends, and I was not dressed up at all. One of my girlfriends pushed me out in the aisle when the emcee asked who wanted to come down. I got onstage to sing, and I won a second prize of five dollars and tickets to the theater. That was a great night. My grandmother also enrolled me and Louise in tap dance at the Sadie Bruce Tap Dance School because we were always tap-dancing around the house. Sadie Bruce operated her school on Fifty-Fourth and Calumet. Her school gave dance and music training to Black kids in Bronzeville. But I was turned off to dance because the teacher put us up against the wall and pulled our legs up next to our ears—cold turkey. They grabbed Louise's and my legs with no stretching or anything. It was very painful. We were determined not to ever go back there, so Grandmother let us quit!

When it came to singing, though, I kept going. I would go down to the Harvest Moon Festival in Chicago as a teen. The

Harvest Moon Festival was where Grammy Award–winning singer Eydie Gormé and her husband, Steve Lawrence, got their start. There were over two hundred folks signed up for amateur night, and I was number 135. I kept going to the bathroom to practice. When it was my turn to sing, the judge with the bell looked at me. I think I may have gotten out two lines when—*DING*—he rang the bell. Still, I mustered up the courage to return the next year.

As I held the microphone when I got up to sing the next time, I noticed it was shaking. I couldn't figure out why until I looked down at my hands—it was me. The shaking took over so bad, it crept up into my voice. I was convinced the bell was going to ring, so I kept my eye on the bell man the whole time. He had the bell in his hand but never rang it. He let me sing the whole song. But I knew it wasn't because I was good—he probably thought that if he rang the bell, I was going to have a heart attack.

Despite my nervousness, I kept at it for a while. But it was hard for me to just let go and sing because I was so inhibited. Kids made fun of me all the time in the neighborhood, calling me knock-a-dock and beanpole because I was skinny and knock-kneed. Instead of crying, I decided to laugh when they made fun of me. It worked, because after a while they didn't find it fun to tease me anymore. I took that power from them, but my confidence took a big hit. In fact, it went into the toilet. You never forget things like that. I don't know why they stick, but I have never forgotten what those kids said. I found it best to keep the dream of singing, or anything else for that matter, to myself. In some cases, I just stopped dreaming altogether.

When it came to a social life, I was invisible at school. I was not part of any club or sport. You would have thought I would have been interested in acting, but that never occurred to me. I did discover I was very good with accents. I could emulate the accents of any of my foreign teachers to a T. I didn't have much of a social life out of school either; in fact, none of us did, because the numbers business was being run out the house. We couldn't answer the phone, have company, or even go out during that time, so we could not have regular teenage lives.

Susie and I were pretty unhappy about it, and eventually we left. I went back to Chicago, and Susie went back to the east side of Detroit with family and friends, while Louise, who was eighteen by that time, went off to get married. Frieda stayed behind in Detroit with Mother.

Going back to Chicago was different. My father wasn't there anymore. He had died in 1947, when I was sixteen. I don't know how he died. All I heard was that he had a hernia. He'd been sickly just before then.

I carried a lot of guilt after his death, because my father came to me the night before he went to the hospital. I was asleep in my room, and he came in and asked me to rub his back because it hurt. I remember I started rubbing it and fell back asleep.

When I woke up, he was at the hospital, where he passed away. I didn't go to the funeral because I wanted to remember my father like he was when he was alive. I'm glad I didn't go, because I heard there were women trying to climb into his casket—and that would have traumatized me more. Anyway, my father was gone. When I left my mother's house in Detroit to go back to Chicago, it no longer felt like home with him gone.

Before my father died, he told me I had a little sister named Rosemary. I started going to visit Rose, who was four years old. My neighborhood friend and eventual husband, Buddy, had a niece named Cookie, who was five. I loved picking them up and taking them places. I would take them to movies and to see Santa Claus during Christmas and things like that.

When Dad died, it didn't even cross my mind to go down to the basement for the box of money he'd hidden for us. By the time I remembered it, my grandmother had already taken the box away, and the space where it had been was now empty. I heard her say, "This is my house, and everything in here is mine." That meant I had no inheritance from my father. We grew up shortly after the 1929 Depression, so people didn't trust the banks and kept their life savings tucked away somewhere at home. She took whatever was there.

Back in Chicago, I decided to finish school at Wendell Phillips High. I had gone to St. Elizabeth's previously, but the nuns there were known for being very strict, and that had been my experience too. I felt that one of the nuns in particular was targeting me. I loved English and was good at it. The final straw was when six book reports were due, and I turned in five of them early. For the sixth one I chose a book that was not on her list. For this the nun ignored the other five book reports I turned in and failed me. I decided to switch to Wendell Phillips High School, where they let me take two English classes, and I graduated from there.

As it turns out, there were a lot of notable artists who went to Wendell Phillips. Their pictures now hang in the school's hallway. Folks like Dinah Washington, Sam Cooke, Herbie Hancock, and Nat King Cole, and I'm proud to say that my picture hangs among them.

I said earlier that I loved English, and that's because of the education I got when I was younger. I'd attended Douglas Elementary School and really liked my teachers. I was never the class clown, but I was the kid who always got caught talking. Someone would eventually turn around and say something to me, and I'd answer them and then get in trouble. As a result, I'd be in the cloak room with tape on my mouth.

Or I was put out in the hall so that when the principal walked by, he could see me. He'd come to me and say, "Now, you're not gonna be out here tomorrow, are you?"

"No," I'd reply. But I'd be out there the next day, and he stopped asking after a while. Most of the time, it was because somebody was talking to me, and I didn't have enough sense not to answer.

When Louise and I were in elementary school, my grandmother convinced my father to send us to a Catholic boarding school. She told him we were too much to handle and thought the discipline would be good for us. Hattie called my mother and asked her to come to town to help convince my father. I didn't know that, but I felt sure she would be on our side about not going. We were skating outside, and I kept rolling by to hear my mother and father arguing. I was hoping my father would win, but he finally gave in. Off we went to Sisters of the Good Shepherd Boarding School. Part of the deal was that my mother had to enroll my younger sister Frieda. My father said, "You put my kids in boarding school, then you're sending her too." The students called us the Three Little Sisters, after a popular song. One day my sisters and I were outside walking and talking, and the nuns ran out to get us because they were afraid we were going to escape through the gate. They separated us so we could never be together outside again. I thought nuns were supposed to be happy because they are married to Christ. But I discovered many of them were angry and mean. I also saw how they mistreated a couple of orphan white kids who had been there for a while. They would grab them by their hair and were verbally abusive. I remember one student who seemed mildly mentally disabled always being the object of the nuns' bullying. I was glad when a Black couple adopted this little white girl named Mary Lou who we liked. We were all happy to see her get a home. I hope she did well.

Some of my fondest memories of boarding school were the visits from Father Ernest, who was the priest at Corpus Christi Catholic Church. He would come once a month and talk to us. We liked Father Ernest because he was kind.

While I enjoyed his talks, there were a lot of Catholic teachings that didn't sit well with me. I would be in church, and the priest would say that if babies died before being baptized, they would stay in limbo. Adults were in purgatory. I didn't believe that. I was in church one day, and the priest said, "Aren't you happy you are Catholic and you are saved? You know, we're the only ones who are saved." I heard my Spirit say, *That's not true.* I said to myself, *Don't say that. Listen to the priest.* But what my Spirit was telling me felt true.

After school I would often go to Olivet Baptist Church, a community center around the corner from our house on the South Side. They had a counselor there named Jim Brown. He would take us to his house and give us Cokes, cookies, and sandwiches. Sometimes he'd take the boys on the field to play baseball. We went to other areas of the city, where they played other teams. If the boys won, we'd have to be prepared to run, because the girls from the rival school would want to beat us up. Although my childhood was filled with mistreatment and disappointments from my family, there were people around us and in our community who were kind to me, and I'll never forget them.

I had a big crush on a boy called Buddy, who lived across the street from me from the time I was nine years old. His real name was Jordan Joseph Gibbs. Everybody knew I liked him, including him, yet the feeling was not mutual. He was two years older than me and was the cutest boy in the neighborhood. He reminded me of a movie star (as time went on, he didn't seem anything like one). Buddy lived with his mother and two sisters, Pearl and Barbara. They were very poor, and I think he was always ashamed of that. Because Buddy was quiet, it was easy for me to imagine he was thinking of me or whatever worked in my fantasy. I imagined that he really liked me, but he couldn't say it because he was shy.

But Buddy actually kissed my older sister, Louise. I remember hearing that one of Buddy's friends told him he should date my sister because when he kissed her, she closed her eyes. When my turn came for Buddy to kiss me, my eyes were wide open. Bright-eyed and bushy-tailed, I wanted to witness every moment of my dream becoming a reality.

As we grew up, Buddy would show me a little attention from time to time and then would act jealous if someone showed that they cared about me.

Of course, that was all I needed to stay enamored.

When we became teenagers, my girlfriends would hang out at my house, and from my porch we could see upstairs into the window where the boys hung out at Buddy's house. We would get tired of them not giving us attention, so we came up with all kinds of pranks to bust up their games. One time we called the police and acted like we were nosy neighbors who were concerned about these guys playing cards while a dead body lay there. We waited for the police to come and then watched the boys panic. Of course, there was no dead body, so the police left. We met the guys outside and pretended we were concerned. "What happened?" we all asked with straight faces. We got what we wanted, which was the boys outside paying attention to us—at least for ten minutes. Then they went right back upstairs. We were so bad back then. In retrospect, that was a dangerous prank and would be even more so now with all the police shootings. Back then we had a pretty good relationship with a lot of police in the community. We had both Black and white cops walking our neighborhoods. And we knew most of them by name. In fact, one police officer was a white man named Billy. He would help us cross the street and was kind to us, so I'd bring him an apple sometimes. It was a time when police walked through the community and cared about the people who lived there. At least, that's what I experienced in my neighborhood.

Another time we called the boys while they were playing

cards and pretended to be sexy women who liked them. In our most seductive voices, we said, "We saw you hanging out at your job and would like to meet you." They were seventeen by this time and so gullible. They asked how we looked, and we said, "Well, I don't like to brag, but I have long hair, and people say I have pretty legs." They got so excited. We made up a fake address out of the local area where they could meet these imaginary foxy ladies. They called a cab and ran out to wait for it. While they were waiting, we went outside and asked them, "Where are y'all going?" Of course they lied to us.

We just smiled and watched them hop in the cab, off to nowhere. When the cab was out of sight, we fell out and couldn't stop laughing. When the guys came back with frowns on their faces, we asked, "What happened?" But we knew exactly what happened . . . nothing!

Eventually Buddy started liking one of the girls in our neighborhood. She was a foster child who lived down the street from me. I remember the day he walked past me, eating ice cream with her. It hurt, but I never said a word. After all, I wasn't his girlfriend, just a girl with a crush. He later told me he was with her because I wasn't the kind of girl who has sexual intercourse, and he was right; I was a virgin. But he was my childhood crush, and I liked him, so when I turned eighteen and Buddy asked if I would have sex with him, I said yes. Then I dodged him for the longest. It had been my goal to wait until I was married to have sex. At boarding school, Father Ernest told us to draw a circle around ourselves and let no one in. In retrospect, he was telling us to keep ourselves protected. I wanted to do that; however, I also wanted to keep Buddy's attention.

When we grew older, Buddy would take on other personalities and names, and with these personas came great accomplishments and great stories . . . Another way of putting it is, Buddy became a compulsive liar. I understand now that he was reaching to be so much more than who he believed he was.

He was boasting about himself, but if you were looking close, you could see the sadness and insecurity in his eyes. Of course, when you're young you usually don't know how to look that deep; all I saw was that he was cute and quiet. Buddy also had a mean streak. He teased other boys to make them feel small, and still that didn't deter me.

One day we ended up at his house while his mother was gone, and we had sex—or at least tried to. He didn't know what the hell he was doing, and neither did I, so nothing really happened. It just wound up being a painful experience. What I didn't know was that this was a preview of coming attractions.

I had a good friend named Ruth Quiñones, whose son would grow up to be well-known as Shabba Doo, the creator of pop locking and star of the classic movie *Breakin'*! Back then Ruth was like a sister to me, and I listened to her. So when she told me—no, encouraged me—to have sex, I was intrigued. Ruth said, "Girl, when you look in the mirror after sex, you'll be glowing!" She was having sex and describing in great detail how wonderful it was. Let me tell you, the whole seventeen years I was married to Buddy, "wonderful" never happened. I waited and waited and eventually convinced myself that Ruth and the other folks who said they loved sex were lying. *They ain't feeling nothing*, I said to myself.

See, I had a selfish lover in Buddy, who was also a premature ejaculator. Back then I didn't know what that was, and neither did he. Neither of us was a communicator; in fact, I was super shy and timid, especially around sex. So we never discussed it, and I didn't discuss it with anyone else. To top it off, Buddy was a hit-it-and-quit-it lover, so when he was done . . . it was done. He was not only unable to wait long enough for me to be pleased, but he didn't seem to care. I didn't think you could have kids if you didn't feel anything, but I was wrong. There was no pleasure or orgasms, but I did end up with two beautiful sons.

A while after our first sexual fiasco, Buddy got with a girl who had formerly lived in Chicago. I knew her cousins; in fact, her older cousin lived in my grandmother's basement, and the others lived a few blocks away. She was a Latina who was pretty and sexy, with long hair. We had all seen her in the newspaper as a model. When she returned to town, she had a three-year-old daughter. Buddy started dating her, and of course this broke my heart. Our friends in the neighborhood were upset that I was hurt, but I didn't want them to have hard feelings toward her. So I went to Buddy's house and congratulated him on his new love. When I walked away that day, I thought that was the end of us.

Buddy was drafted into the Marines during the Korean War. While he was there, the Marines got a letter from his girlfriend saying she was pregnant. They sent him home to take care of the complaint. Buddy called to tell me what happened and asked me what I thought he should do. I told him, "I think you should do what you feel." His mother and father were happy with his girlfriend; they loved the way she looked. Buddy decided marrying her was the right thing. Convincing myself that I was truly over him and of course diminishing my own hurt, I decided to throw them a party. Now I was sure it was the end of us!

My very first job was for a fur-grooming-and-storage company. I made fifty cents an hour as a telephone solicitor whose job was to sell storage to customers who owned fur coats. Part of my pitch was to tell the customers that their furs were locked in a refrigerated room and were cleaned and glazed. One day I went and looked in the storage room and realized the owner had us lying. The furs were sitting in a hot room and not being taken care of at all! I didn't like lying to the customers, and some of the other workers felt the same way. We started improvising the script, and every time the boss came out to check on us, one of us would call his office and send him back to answer the phone. It was so funny. Eventually I grew tired of it. It just didn't feel right, so I left.

When I started looking for work, I was having a hard time during the interview process, because when they'd ask if I had any experience, I would always answer, "No, but I'm willing to learn." I thought that would impress them. It didn't. I was a fast learner and I was willing to work hard, so having no experience didn't seem like an obstacle to me. As you might guess, they saw it differently. My girlfriend Ruth, always the one with advice, said, "Girl, let me show you how to find a job." She told me the first rule during an interview is LIE! That's right; lie about everything except operating a power machine. Ruth also told me I would have to jump in front of the other applicants before they jumped in front of me, in case there was only one opening. Most of our job hunting was in the garment district. We would go in and sort of investigate what the job entailed, so when we applied, we could say we knew how to do it. At one job the main duty was to run a button machine. The manager asked, "Have you operated a button machine before?" Ruth said, "Yes." He told her to turn it on. When she couldn't figure it out, he said, "You turn it on over here." Ruth replied, "Oh, the one I learned on, the switch was on the other side." They would hire Ruth on the spot, but she wouldn't take the job. She was just teaching me the ropes and showing me how to play the game.

My next job was at the Guggenheimer Corporation. The seamstresses would use chalk to mark where they were going to sew. My job was to wipe the chalk off; that's it. There was a lady who worked there, and I've never forgotten her. They fired her one day. The next day the lady clocked in and went to work. They said, "You're fired. You don't work here anymore." She ignored them and kept on working. When the manager removed her time card, this lady made her own time card and put it in the time clock. She was still working there when I left. I mean to tell you, that lady was not about to let them fire her!

I was in the middle of looking for my next job when I was put out of my grandmother's house. I was a huge lover of animals, especially dogs and cats. Anyone who knew me knew that. I had picked up a stray puppy, and when the puppy went missing, I went to the pound to look for him, but he wasn't there. A worker there told me that all the dogs in this certain cage would be killed in five days. They were supposed to be vicious, but all of them were jumping up and down, begging me to take them. So I asked for them all. Can you imagine what would have happened if he had given them to me? Thankfully the worker told me I could only choose one. So I chose the dog I was sure nobody would want. When I got home, my grandmother opened the door and said, "That's not the puppy you lost!" I confessed that I didn't find the puppy, but this one was going to be killed if I didn't take it. My grandmother said she didn't care. "You and that dog can both leave," she declared, and so we did.

I called my girlfriend Claire, whom I had already given a dog to, and we moved in together. So there we were, two girls with two dogs in one room. Oh, I should mention that we were also living in the room next to the landlord. Claire and I both loved animals, so when a cat with a busted eye came to our window, we started feeding him. I took the cat to a vet, but I had no money. The vet showed me all the animals that people left and never came back for. So back home I went with the cat. We left him outside to avoid getting on the bad side of the landlord. But he was on to us though and warned that if we didn't get rid of the dogs, we would have to leave. As difficult as it was for us to do so, we got rid of the dogs. To our further disappointment, the landlord still put us out!

I still hadn't found a job, so Claire let me stay with her at a new place she'd found. Claire eventually left to live with her sister, and since I couldn't afford to keep the room alone, the landlord allowed me to stay on their couch. But they made it very hard for me. Every night, when I was trying to sleep, the family would stay in the living room and talk over me. I got the message loud and clear that they wanted me gone . . . so I left.

I had started attending Cortez W. Peters Business School

to learn typing and shorthand; there, I met another student named Faye Raye. She was friends with the manager of the Pershing Hotel, and she talked him into renting me a room for nine dollars a week. So that was my next move. I still wasn't working yet and needed money to be able to stay there. When my father died, he left money for my sister Louise and I, but my grandmother wasn't a fair woman—at least not with me. She made sure Louise got her money and that I didn't get a dime. To add insult to injury, she was also not sharing money from his ice business or his mechanic shop with me. I have to say, it hurt that Louise didn't stand up for me or even share any of her money from Dad either. But you start out the way you will end, and unfortunately my sister would always be in need of money.

Years later, when I was on television, Louise needed help. I didn't hesitate to help, because as they say, "Success is the best revenge." I brought her out here to LA and bought her a home. She made her transition here, and to be honest, it did my heart good to know she loved living out here.

Anyway, back then I was growing tired of them stealing my share of my father's inheritance from me, and I came up with an idea. I would sit in my father's business and wait for the mechanic to collect money from his customers, and when he did, my hand would be right there! That's how I paid for the hotel. Faye became a great friend, probably the best friend I'd had up to this point. Most of my friends took me for granted and would say I was a "sucker" or "too nice" behind my back. One of those friends, Loretta, almost got me kicked out of the hotel. I had a bad habit of trying to save people who didn't want to be saved. Enter Loretta, who was a girl who had family issues. I understood what it was like to feel unwanted, so I let her come stay in the hotel room with me. Each day that I left for school, Loretta pretended to get dressed to job hunt. I had even researched leads for her, but as soon as I left, Loretta would put on a robe and walk down the halls of the hotel, meeting people. Apparently she was looking for a different kind of job.

One day she lied and told me that she had paid the rent, so I bought a pair of shoes. The hotel manager confronted me, and that's when I learned what Loretta was doing and that, of course, she had not paid the rent. The hotel manager let me stay, but he raised the rent on me, even though I put Loretta out.

Faye Raye was different. She was a giver and would secretly slip money into my pocket if she knew I was low, or sometimes she would buy food and pretend she didn't want it so she could give it to me. Faye moved to New York and became a dancer. She was a sensation, dancing at the Cotton Club and the Apollo, and in the chorus for Cab Calloway, Duke Ellington, and so many other jazz greats. While she was touring with a dance group, Faye came to Detroit. I was so delighted to see her. After that, we lost track of each other. But years later, when I went to New York to do *The Vagina Monologues* with Lainie Kazan, I found Faye, and we remained close until she passed.

Before I could graduate from business college, I landed a job at Service Bindery. I figured everything I was learning in school I was already doing there, so I dropped out. I had a habit of hooking my friends up whenever I got a job. So, at Service Bindery I got my sister Louise and my friend Laura hired. But before I could get anyone else hired, Mr. Berman, one of the owners, let me know, "We didn't need you when we hired you . . . but your application was so good, I couldn't afford not to hire you."

That let me know to stop trying to pull anyone else in. At Service Bindery our job was basically to take easels and run them through a glue machine so that cardboard displays could be attached.

Around this time I was about twenty years old, and in my free time I hung out at a local bar. I got involved with a young man named Burgess, who loved to tease me, and even though he got on my nerves, I liked him. Eventually we started dating, and I wound up pregnant. Burgess's response was the same old routine most guys used: "How do I know it's mine?" I was hurt and clearly on my own.

I was still new to Service Bindery, and it was a good job. When I realized I was pregnant, I was afraid that my boss would fire me when he found out. That was a hard time for me. I was Catholic and believed that abortion was a sin. But I was also broke and terrified of having a baby alone. Back then abortions were dangerous, so we had to buy concoctions from the pharmacy and pray that they worked. In my case it did. That's why today I am in support of women having a choice. And a place where they can get the proper medical care. I struggled so much during that time; if I had had a place to go to get counseled and properly treated, I wouldn't have been so afraid. You have to walk a mile in someone else's shoes to understand what they're going through.

Service Bindery turned out to be a great job. I got promoted early. First I was assisting the guy in charge of the mail. One day he came in pretty hungover. Every time Mr. Berman came looking for him, he was in the bathroom. When he came out, Mr. Berman asked him, "Have you been drinking?" His response was that he only had a couple of beers. The third time Mr. Berman came looking for him and saw that he was back in the bathroom, he turned to me and asked, "Can you do this job?" I answered, "YES!" So it was mine.

I got the idea to buy a notebook and start recording every stamp and every label that went on a package. What I was doing was simple, but it had never been done before at Service Bindery. Mr. Berman found it extremely helpful and was very proud. In fact, he would call me into his office and say, "Margaret, bring your book!" And then, in front of the client, he would ask, "How many pieces were used for this job, and what was the postage?" We had clients like *Esquire*, *Life* magazine, and other popular organizations, and as it turns out, my new system was used to validate the shipping costs.

There were two owners at Service Bindery: Mo Berman and Jack Goldman. Mo ran the factory, and Jack brought in the clients. Mo was bragging about me in the mail room and gave Jack the idea to steal me and put me on the switchboard in the office. I was being fought over, and it felt good. The two owners continued to argue, until one day Jack Goldman came to me and asked, "Do you want to work in the office?" I said yes. He told me to get up right then and there, and took me to the switchboard. "Sit down," he said. And that ended the feud between them.

Jack had wanted me in the office from the beginning, but I didn't know how to run the switchboard and told him so. Chile . . . if my friend Ruth had heard me, she would have killed me for not lying. So, my girlfriend Laura, whom I'd helped get the job, was the first to work in the office, because she did lie when they asked her. There had never been a Black woman working in the office before. Everyone who was Black worked in the factory, as with most jobs back then. We had an office manager named Edna Shankins and a bookkeeper named Delores. Edna was racist and thought she was slick. She would make little derogatory comments or digs about Black people and then pretend to be innocent. Laura wasn't having it. When I started working in the office, Laura had already started getting on Edna's case. She wouldn't let Edna get away with nothing! One day I was laughing so hard at Laura, I had to go down to the bottom drawer of my desk so I couldn't be seen. What happened was, Edna said she had gone downtown and gotten some wonderful nuts. "Let's see," she said. "I got some cashews, almonds, some nigger toes, and pecans. Oh, they were so good."

Laura looked over at me as if to say, *I'm gonna get her.*

"So, Edna," Laura said, "what kind of toes did you say?"

Edna said, "Huh?"

Laura continued, "You said there were some kind of toes, didn't you?"

"No!" Edna answered. She ran down the list again, but this time instead of "nigger toes," Edna called them "Brazil nuts," which is the correct name. But Laura wouldn't let up; she stayed on her case ALL day. Edna had to take breaks and leave the office just to get away, but as soon as she returned, Laura would start again. "I'm still trying to find out what kind of toes you had. I may want to get me some." Edna never tried that mess again, because Laura had taught her a lesson.

Jack Goldman had a son named Allen, who was my supervisor in the mail room. We realized we had a lot in common and enjoyed each other's company. Allen started bringing me lunch every day. He even brought a hot plate to the office so he could cook me ravioli. Allen was falling for me. He was good-looking, about twenty-three years old, kind, and funny. Truth be told, I was falling for him too. There was one problem: Allen was married. I hadn't experienced much kindness from men up to this point, so this feeling was new to me, but it was complicated. He was not only married; he was also the boss's son. I lied to Allen, hoping to end anything before it began. I told him my folks were prejudiced. I thought that would back him off.

Allen went to my grandmother's house and talked to her and my aunt. They both liked him, and Allen couldn't wait to tell me that they were fine with us being together. Of course, he probably didn't mention he was married. My grandmother and aunt loved white folks. To them, white was right. I could not believe Allen had done that. The next excuse I tried was that I was Catholic. Allen wanted us to talk to the priest, but I said, "No!" Allen was persistent, and his persistence won. We started seeing each other, and although I loved being with him, I was always looking for a way out. One day Allen and I got into an argument, and I stopped talking to him. Since he was my boss and I refused to answer him, Allen sent me home. I took it as being fired, so I called the office and asked them to send me my last check. Mr. Goldman got on the phone and told me I needed to come into the office and pick it up.

When I got there, Mr. Goldman had two chairs facing

each other and sat Allen and I both down. He asked, "Now, what's wrong with you two?" At that moment I realized his father knew about us. Allen and I started taking up for each other.

I said, "Well, he is my boss, and I should have answered him."

Then Allen said, "Well, I really shouldn't have sent her home."

This went on until his father looked at us and said, "Both of you go upstairs and get back to work." So that was that. We were together for two years, and during that time I heard that my name came up at Allen's dinner table, so I knew his wife also knew about us. I didn't feel good about it, and I knew I was going to have to end it. She wanted to adopt a baby, and I knew I had to get out of the way.

The Black people who worked in the factory threw a party, and Allen and his brother came. Allen was very popular with the Black employees. Around this time a friend of mine's boyfriend introduced me to his cousin. Harvey was his name, and all I can say is, the man was fine, fine, fine! Harvey came to pick me up from the party, and Allen begged me not to leave with him. I said, "I've got to go. Plus, you and your wife are planning to adopt a kid. You two will make it." His brother told him to let me go. Allen was about to cry. I knew if I left with Harvey, it would be goodbye, so I left.

Harvey was attractive on the outside, but inside he was

tormented. For a long time, I didn't realize Harvey was on heroin. He had a way of not coming around when he was high. He would clean up and then start coming around again. Harvey dropped by one day and was itching so bad, he couldn't stop scratching. He told me he ate something bad, and I bought his lie. I was twenty-two and naive about a lot of things. But Harvey could get mean too.

Funny thing is that he took to calling me Princess Margaret, like my father had. But he usually said it in a sarcastic tone, and I got the sense that he thought that I was better than him. Men and their egos. Buddy had similar issues of feeling less than, as his family's lack of money and possessions affected his self-esteem.

One day Harvey and I were on the phone, and again he was insulting me. I told him I was going to hang up. He said, "You better not," but I did. Next thing I knew, Harvey was at my apartment. I lived upstairs, over the landlord, who was sitting on the porch. When Harvey arrived, he said, "I told you not to hang up," and started beating me up.

I hollered for help, but the landlord didn't hear me. I managed to get away from Harvey and get downstairs where the landlord was, and I told him, "I want him to leave." Harvey left, and as he did, he turned and gave me a piercing look. I knew that was the end of our four-month relationship. Shortly after, I discovered I was pregnant. When I told Harvey, I heard the same old line again: "How do I know it's mine?" I decided to keep the baby because I'd already had an abortion and didn't want to relive that. In my mind, the baby would be for me. Harvey never acknowledged our daughter, Angela, and my pride wouldn't let me ask him for a dime.

The frequent absences and distance from my mother and grandmother affected me in many ways, including the way I yearned so for a connection with women friends and family. Maybe too much, given how often I was mistreated by friends. I had a girlfriend who was like a sister to me—or so I thought. We had so much fun and went through so much together, making many lasting memories. We lived together two or three times. I got her a job at Service Bindery when I worked there.

But there were times when she did hurtful things. She turned off the alarm clock so that I would oversleep, and then she sat at the window at work so she could laugh as she watched me running to the building. I dismissed it. Took it on the chin. Laughed about it. I would save money out of each check and put it in a piggy bank. I would eat beans and make sacrifices to save my money. She ate steak and laughed at me. I discovered later that that was funny to her because she paid for the steak with the money she stole out of my piggy bank. I didn't have the backbone back then to confront her. I lacked the self-worth.

When I was married to Buddy, his sister wanted some money, and my friend told her, "Let's make up a story and tell Dimples. She's a sucker and will fall for anything." Buddy was present, but they waited for him to leave before they carried out the plan.

Long after that incident, my sister-in-law told the story to Buddy and some friends of how they'd tricked me out of my money. They laughed in my face, and it hurt. I couldn't believe this was supposed to be my close friend. It was then that I realized she was not a friend at all.

When I asked my mother why she was like that, Mother said, "Listen, God is taking care of you. You are never without a job, and you're able to take care of yourself. People like that will always be looking for something; they will always need something." Years later, when I was on TV, this friend would ask to come to the show and would brag to her friends about me. I was polite and gracious, but I was never close to her again.

My grandmother died when I was pregnant with my daughter Angela. She passed away when I moved to Detroit to live with my mother. I didn't have any feelings when she died, unlike most people do when they lose their grandmother. We didn't have a close or loving relationship. And yet I'm still having conversations with her in my head. Growing up, I didn't have a close relationship with my mother either because she wasn't there. I had to learn how to be a woman and a mother the best way I could—mostly from reading and movies. Who would have thought back then that my daughter and I would make our living from stories on an electronic screen—big or small? Or that pursuing a creative passion would help us to heal from the bites that life took out of our hearts and minds? I didn't have anyone to sit me down and explain the facts of life or how to be a woman. I remember that when my period came, I was riding a bike, and I saw the blood. I didn't even know what it was. My grandmother and aunt told me "this" was going to happen every month, and they didn't want anybody to know when I was on my period. They cut up rags, and that's what I had to wear during my cycle. We couldn't go buy Kotex because my grandmother and aunt were old-fashioned. Instead I had to wash those rags out every month. It was a horrible time.

I was closer with my younger sister Frieda than I was with a lot of women in my life. The opportunity to spend more time with her was one of my motivations for moving from Chicago to Detroit.

Frieda made her own world. I loved and admired her for that. A real beauty, she and her friends entered beauty contests. She found an opportunity to model. Frieda could wake up from sleeping, slide out of the bed in the morning, and never have to make up the bed. She was so smooth. It was like she hadn't been in it.

She was exceptional among women in the 1950s, who for the most part did what was expected of girls and women, and that was to limit their ambitions and dreams to marrying well and having children. During the early 1940s, when men were away fighting in World War II in great numbers, the job market had opened up for women, out of necessity. You might have outwardly been pursuing a BS or BA in college, but that was to meet the man who would bestow on you the Mrs. In the postwar years, women were being discouraged from having the independence they had during the war, when the local labor forces were deprived of male workers. You were considered an old maid if you weren't married past your early twenties. I didn't go after the college degrees, but I did get the Mrs.

Our culture and systems of law discouraged and blocked women from owning real estate, businesses, and such. We were not allowed checking accounts or credit cards. We were passed over for inheritances in favor of male heirs. So when women such as my sister and our mother worked around the obstacles and broke through barriers, it was by the force of their will and determination. Necessity can give you courage where it may not otherwise be easy to summon.

My move to Detroit as a young woman put me closer to my sister and mother. I now had a chance to deepen my relationship with them. Mother and Frieda had had more time together than I had with either of them separately or together. I now had the opportunity to talk to my mother about how I grew up. We were able to share our respective thoughts about life. We had a lot of catching up to do. I was able to hear Mother's side of what happened between her and my dad and his mother. My paternal grandmother was the domineering mom who believed her son could do no wrong and the child bride he'd moved into her home could do no right. My mother had no one to protect her nor defend her when my father was abusive. Him hitting her was more than she was willing to take. She said that she had to get away, and I understood why. Most important, I came to see that the distance created between us was no reflection of her lack of love for her children—my sister and me—even though Frieda did join her, earlier than I did. I envied that. But there were things I didn't know about their relationship too. Having more time together didn't mean that my sister and mother got along better with each other than they did with me.

After my father, my mother did take chances on love again. And she made an effort to keep at least one of her children close. As Frieda was growing up, my mother took her everywhere she went, even when she was socializing. The next major relationship Mother had after Father was with Chester Rentie. If my mother went out clubbing with Mr. Rentie, they brought Frieda along. As children are wont to do, Frieda grew attached to Mr. Rentie, such that when Mr. Rentie and Mother separated and she told Frieda that from now on it was going to be just the two of them, my sister was upset.

There are many things Frieda experienced that she still has a hard time recovering from. When one of Mother's boyfriends got in the bed with her, Frieda moved into a hotel, one that our mother owned. Frieda never told our mother what her man had done. She was afraid our mother would kill the man. So she kept the secret—for a while.

She and Mama would later argue, and the truth would come out. Things got ugly and out of hand. Frieda gave Mother some lip, and my mother put a gun in Frieda's mouth and threatened to blow her brains out. Frieda was traumatized, of course. She never got over it. She just cut our mother out of her life completely.

I've always felt that Frieda didn't continue therapy long enough to work through it.

I encouraged Frieda to work things out with Mother. Frieda did seek counseling. From that time on, when we girls got together with our mother, Frieda would join in the conversations with the three of us for a bit. But she'd soon make her way toward the door and disappear. She avoided talking to Mother altogether. She never forgave her, and apparently her takeaway from counseling was that it's okay to hate your mother. I think at times when Frieda was hurtful to me, it was because I reminded her of Mother, whom she so deeply resented. I'm always trying to help people, and that would get on Frieda's nerves, because that's how Mother was.

I tried to maintain a closeness to my aunt Vera, and it

seemed to go well for a while. She would call me as soon as I arrived home from work and give me the run-down on what was going wrong in her life. Mostly she complained about what her husband was doing, and I felt obligated to listen. Meanwhile, my son Joey (what we called my son Jordan), a little one then, would cry because I would be on the phone for hours. I'd shoo him away, telling him to go outside and play. When we know better, we do better.

One of the best things to happen in those years was that my mother and her granddaughter—my firstborn, Angela—really bonded. Mother took the opportunity to be nurturing to Angela. She would call Angela "my darling" and put her in bed with her. I was barely given time to play with my own child. And when they were together, my mother wouldn't put her down. So much so that I became a bit jealous, to tell you the truth.

My daughter got from my mother what I did not. As only grandmothers can do, my mother interfered with my authority as a parent. Angela would say she didn't want to eat because her food had gotten cold, and I would say, "It was hot when I gave it to you. I don't care if there are icicles on it; you have to lick them off and then eat it." Here would come my mother saying, "Maybe she doesn't feel well." Angela would sit there, looking from me to my mother to see who was going to win. As soon as I gave her "the look," she would eat.

My mother lived a life of great ups and downs, but she was something special, a star in her realm throughout her life. She attracted other people who were the same. She was given the name Princess Ophelia, not for nothing. She became a member of a church led by the Reverend James Francis Jones. Jones was a charismatic spiritual leader in the tradition of others such as Daddy Grace, Father Divine, and Reverend Ike. The church had its own holiday to replace Christmas. Philamathy, I'm told it was called. The festivities began on his birthday, November 24, and went for eight days. I knew only a bit about him at the time but have learned more in recent years.

He owned and wore the finest of things and favored wearing green because "it's the color of money." Being based in the Midwest, where we have some wicked winters, allowed for excesses in his clothing. He was known for "a velvet-lined white mink coat, a gold-handled cane, and a jewel-encrusted turban," according to an article in a Detroit paper. He, like my mother, was known for having the gift of sight.

He bestowed titles onto his inner circle. People were Prince, Princess, Lord, Lady. He called his fully staffed mansion "the Castle." My mother became Princess Ophelia. So I was not the first in the family to be called Princess. As you can imagine, I was far from living the life of a princess or wearing the clothes of one, while my mother was written up in the local papers as one of Detroit's best dressed. She was an original. I'm an original. We all are.

Mother had a small hotel by that time with four rooms. I stayed there and earned my keep ironing sheets. My younger sister, Frieda, would ask, "Why are you doing all this?" and my reply was always the same: "She is not the father of this baby." I worked there because I didn't want to be living off of my mother. I wanted to be independent. Money came to me in other ways as well. I was in a car accident and sued for $50,000. I got a judgment in my favor, but by the time we got through paying the attorneys and doctors, I got about $1,600 out of it. I intended to save that money for my daughter in case something happened to me. Then one day my mother's older sister, my aunt Margaret, who I'm named after, called me and said she needed to borrow some money. I denied her, sharing that I was holding the money for Angela's needs. My mother overheard part of the conversation, then asked further what it was that Margaret wanted. I told her, and Mother said, "I was about to say, because you're over here living off of me." I was shocked. She broke my heart with that response. I was doing everything I could not to be a burden to her, and it appeared that she hadn't noticed.

CHAPTER THREE

The Great Escape

We only had four hours to get our belongings and get out of Dodge.

I decided to move Angela and myself back to Chicago. My grandmother was gone, but my aunt Bell was still there. While I worked, she took care of Angela, who was a rambunctious little thing, running us over with her stroller if we weren't careful. It was during my return to Chicago that I started dating Buddy, who I'd had a crush on in childhood. He would come by and pick up Angela while I was at work. They looked alike, and I thought he would make a good father.

My aunt Bell thought so too. Buddy and I were going to premarital classes at the Catholic church, and everything seemed like it was going to be fine. Then one day my girlfriend Laura's husband came to my aunt Bell's with her. His mother had put Laura out, and he'd allowed it to happen. He just looked at me and said, "Here she is." He left Laura there with me, but there was no room for her. We solved that problem by getting an apartment two blocks away. Luckily it was next door to my big sister, Louise, and her family.

Laura and I were still working at Service Bindery and were thick as thieves. Buddy didn't want me to go to the new apartment, but I always looked out for my friends. I felt responsible for them. Eventually Laura's husband, Ernest, and Buddy both moved in with us. It just so happened that Louise and Jimmy's apartment and ours were both on the fourth floor, and our windows were right next to each other. We would pass Angela back and forth to each other through the window. Thank God, we never dropped her. But there was a time when we almost dropped Louise.

She was fighting with her husband, and we were trying to pull her into our window while he was trying to pull her back. We won. Louise eventually got up the courage to fight him back. She hit him with a lamp, and he stopped hitting her.

As for Buddy and me, we were preparing for marriage—or trying to. I didn't get him to counseling. I tried asking him to use protection while we were having sex. I wanted to be married before I had another child. He agreed for a short while. Then he changed his mind. We argued about it. He refused to put on protection and forced himself on me. The consequence of that was our son, my second child, Joey. As soon as Buddy learned that I was pregnant, his general attitude changed, his attitude grew worse, and he felt like now he "had" to marry me.

He began to think, more than ever, that marriage was the next step we should take. I thought so too, of course, but when our wedding day came, something in me felt hollow. I was unexcited—sad, even.

As we were getting into the cab to go to the church, I felt so clearly that I should not go through with the wedding. I turned to Buddy and said, "Listen, we don't have to do this. I already have one child, and having another doesn't make that much difference."

Buddy looked at me and said, "Girl, get in the car."

In attendance at the wedding was my sister Louise, who was my maid of honor; her husband, Jimmy; Buddy's best man; Buddy; and me. There was no one else in the church except a stranger on the second floor; I'll never know who that was. After the ceremony we went to breakfast, and then my brother-in-law suggested we go home, take naps, and then celebrate that evening. We all went home, and that's exactly where Buddy left me. We waited and waited, but he never came back in time for us to go celebrate. I was so embarrassed and hurt. When he finally came home, I got up and went out to the Club DeLisa alone. I sat there, thinking, *This is my wedding day.* That was the beginning of what would become a very bad marriage. I ignored my gut that day. It was warning me not to marry this man. I did not have enough self-worth to trust my own intuition, and the price I would pay would be heavy.

My marriage was broken from the start, but I wanted to fix it. When I returned from Detroit, I suggested to Buddy that we work the same shifts so we could be home together more. More time together made things worse.

Buddy had a job while I was still working at Service Bindery, but he got laid off. My mother persuaded him to come to Detroit to find work. Buddy and I had an agreement. He was to go to Detroit to look for work, but if he didn't find a job, he was to come back and look in Chicago. Mother convinced Buddy to lie to me and pretend he had a job when he didn't. I quit my job and packed up our place alone while I was pregnant and had a toddler. I moved us to Detroit only to find out Buddy was unemployed. I felt betrayed by both him and Mother. I immediately went out and got a job working as an Addressograph machine operator. I was clear I would not ever have my mother say I was leaning on her with my husband and two kids.

I smoked like a fiend back then. We had no idea that smoking cigarettes caused low birth weights in babies. When Joey was born in 1956, he had to stay in the hospital for two months because he was a preemie. I was not able to hold him and bond with him in the way I wanted to and that he needed. When Joey came home, he was so little that my mother thought something serious was wrong with him.

One day she said to him, "When your mother goes to work, we're going to take you to the hospital." The moment she said that, Joey stood up on his little infant legs while she was holding him. He was like, *Nope, I'm not going back to the hospital.* She laughed and realized that he was fine.

After Joey was born, I landed a job as a switchboard operator at the Gotham Hotel. It was Black-owned and was a hot spot for Black millionaires and Black entrepreneurs. I remember there was a gift shop with fancy jewelry that I loved. The nine-story, two-hundred-room hotel sat at 111 Orchestra Place and had a fancy restaurant, a great brunch, and an all-girls jazz band. I would later emulate that at my jazz club, Marla's Memory Lane.

Anyway, the Gotham Hotel was the pride of Black Detroit, with beautiful archways, paintings on the walls, and big windows adorned with fancy drapes. The millionaires would sit in the lobby, where photos of many of them hung on the wall. They wore suits, starched shirts, and long silk ties. As I was heading in for my shifts, I would see them eating brunch in the gorgeous dining room. The job at the Gotham Hotel was a good one. I got to see a lot of celebrities, like Sammy Davis Jr., who ended up being one of our guest stars on *The Jeffersons* years later. Buddy was jealous and would come down to the hotel and harass me so that I would quit. He would stand outside and spy on me to see if any of the men were trying to hit on me. Finally I agreed to quit, but before I did, he just had to come down and cause a scene. I was furious and told him, "I've already agreed to quit, so please go home!"

Mother was into real estate by this time and helped us buy our first house. She gave us her commission and talked the other Realtor into giving up some of his. I was very excited to have our first home. It was a triplex with a finished basement, and we already had two Jewish tenants.

Since Buddy liked to play cards with his friends, I figured he could host the games at our house sometimes, but he never did. We should have been happy, but it was in that house that the nightmare began. I did things to save money, like wearing knee socks instead of buying stockings, and I did my own hair. I didn't want us arguing over money. Instead of appreciating my sacrifices, Buddy looked at me and said, "Look at you. You're country. Who wants you?"

He was mean and started getting meaner. I was taking care of the bills, and I would get his checks. Buddy had started gambling and one day decided he didn't want me handling his checks anymore. He asked me to give them to him, but I refused because we needed to pay the bills. That was the first time he hit me. He loved saying, "Fuck the bills." I blamed myself for the first hit. *It was his check*, I told myself, *and I should have given it to him.* If a man hits you and you don't address it then, it becomes easier for him to do it again. And that is exactly what happened.

I remember when I had gotten pregnant again, and Buddy and I were arguing. I felt threatened, so I ran out of the house and tripped over a wire around the yard, but I kept on going. I went to my mother's house, but she wasn't home. Buddy came and dragged me out of the bed and made me come back.

I was so stressed that I didn't realize I was miscarrying because of the fall. I was bleeding a lot. Big clots of blood and tissue were sliding out of my body, and I started to hallucinate. I felt like I was trying to get above water but was drowning. Buddy told me to be quiet and go to sleep. I thought to myself, *Never be in trouble with him, because he won't help you.* I kept getting up to go to the bathroom, but each time I would pass out. His sister, Barbara, was staying with us at the time and said, "You better take her to the hospital, because she's turning gray."

I had just bought a new dining room set, and Buddy tried to sit me in one of the chairs, and even in my weakness, I said, "Don't sit me in my new chairs!" He managed to get me in the car. The whole way he was racing to the hospital and giving me updates on where we were because I kept blacking out. As soon as we arrived, the hospital staff saw my condition and started running with me to a room. That scared my husband.

He went straight to my mother's house, and as soon as she saw him, she knew something was wrong. He told her I was in the hospital, and she made her way there. In the meantime, my doctor arrived and saw the nurse trying to unbutton my robe. I vividly remember him saying, "SHIT," and pushing her out the way. He ripped my robe open to check my heartbeat because he couldn't find my pulse. I almost died that night. The doctor performed a D&C procedure to make sure there was no tissue left behind after the miscarriage. I had three miscarriages, but that one was definitely the worst of them all. During another pregnancy, Buddy looked at me and said, "Dimples, I don't want any more babies." I thought to myself, *I'm not doing this alone!* If he was cold enough to tell his pregnant wife he didn't want any more babies, then he should've been smart enough to use a condom. I lost that child too.

Buddy gave me two black eyes during another pregnancy, and I found the courage to leave, so I went to an attorney. He took me to a judge, who asked me how long I'd been married, and I told him, "Four years."

He replied, "Then you ought to know how not to push his buttons." The attorney was very disappointed, and so was I. People often ask why women stay in abusive relationships. It's hard to go when you're broken. Add to that the time I came up in, when women were still considered property and had few rights. Leaving seemed damn near impossible.

My mother tried to help us by giving Buddy a job managing a property of hers. Ever the businessperson, she had by now also become a preacher. She was known as Reverend Princess Ophelia Kemp. When the owner of a local theater began to have trouble, she offered to buy his building. She'd continue to show films there like he did, but she also planned to hold church services there. The property would make for a nice tax write-off. I worked in the box office, a job that worked for me because I was pregnant with Dorian and happy to sit for long periods of time.

Buddy took the job and used his authority to then hire a girlfriend he had on the side to work at my mother's theater. "The box office is her job," he said. I asked him to put her at the candy counter or something. He insisted. There went my comfortable working conditions. I had to go stand at the candy counter in my heels.

I hadn't initially realized that they were an item. But the thought crystallized for me when I saw them together in the box office booth.

One night I came home from work and discovered that I couldn't get in the house. I kept ringing the bell and knocking. I went around to the window and yelled, and nobody woke up. My kids were asleep and didn't hear me.

I called to my neighbor and asked that she call the house, and even then, no one answered the phone. I knew where one of his friends lived, and I went over there to see if he knew where Buddy was. He pretended not to know. I guess he felt sorry for me, because as I was leaving, he said, "Try the Chit Chat Club." That's exactly where I found Buddy, sitting in a booth with the same girl from the theater. I walked up and grabbed him by the shoulder. Buddy said, "Why can't you just sit down like a civilized person?" I told him I needed the key to get in the house, so he gave it to me. I walked across the street alone, got on the bus, and went home.

I did everything I could think of to make the marriage work. I even tried to get him to go to marriage counseling, but Buddy would say, "You're the one who's crazy; you go." Projecting a problem or a flaw you have onto your partner is a common thing people do to avoid the work of healing.

Having lost three opportunities to have another child, I felt like there was a soul out there trying to get through. The next time I was pregnant, I remembered thinking, *Now, whoever this is, they must really want to be here, so please let them come.* My youngest son, Dorian, was born in 1963. On the outside, everything was looking good, but on the inside of that house, there was no happiness. Buddy never wanted to do anything with me or the kids. He never wanted to take me anywhere. Never. One time I gave him the date of when we were going to have a night out together. It was, like, a month away. Every time he wanted to have sex, I'd let him, because I wanted our date night to go smoothly. The night before, I said, "Tomorrow is our date." I could see on his face he didn't want to do it. But I had worked for this. So we went.

He started driving up the block to one of the main streets, but he wasn't slowing down. I thought, *Maybe he's going to a jazz club I've heard about but never been to.* He then went three or four blocks and turned around.

Maybe he's going here, I thought, *or maybe he's going there . . .* This was all going on in my head. Then Buddy went back to the house and pulled up in the driveway and sat, waiting for me to say something. I didn't say a word. He pulled back out. He carried me through a bunch of shit that night. I couldn't believe it. He finally took me to a small club on Linwood. This club had tables with checkered tablecloths. There was a guy performing who was so bad that the owner got up on the stage and took him off. The whole place was awful.

I asked, "Can we go someplace else?"

Buddy said, "I knew you were going to do that!" He had been waiting for me to say something. I asked him why we couldn't go to the club he liked to hang out at. His girlfriend was there, I guessed.

When we got to the club, parking was such that the driver's side was by the curb. Buddy got out of the car, and I sat there. I asked, "Can you open the door for me?"

He said, "So I can get hit by a car?" Apparently he didn't mind if I got hit by one.

So I said, "Take me home. I promise I will never ask you to take me anywhere again in life, okay?"

The abuse didn't stop there. Something happened to Buddy's car, so I offered to take him to work, but he said, "No, I'm taking your car." I was working in downtown Detroit for United Airlines by this time and was given the late shift, so I didn't get off until midnight. It was snowing, and did I mention it was Detroit? Anyway, all my coworkers left, because I told them I had a ride. At about 1:00 a.m., I was still waiting. I called Buddy and said, "Where are you? Aren't you picking me up?"

He said, "It's snowing outside. I'm not coming out there." I had to walk and wait for the bus in the snow, and I was pregnant with my youngest son, Dorian.

That's not someone who cares about you. I couldn't even call my husband a friend with the way he treated me. I thought, *I've known this man since he was eleven years old, and we are no better friends than that?*

For all of my grandmother and Aunt Vera's meanness to me when I was but a child in their care under their roof, now that I was on my own and a young mother, they wanted to tell me how to be and what to do. This may have been their idea of being supportive and loving, but at best they were giving me unsolicited advice and faulty wisdom. Thinking of them reminds me of the saying "The road to hell is paved with good intentions." They talked against breastfeeding, for example. "Mothers don't need to breastfeed because you gotta work. Ain't nobody going to take care of your child if you nurse them," they said.

I knew my mother didn't breastfeed, so I felt guilty even having the desire to. When my daughter was born and I was living with my mother for a short time, she warned me not to pick Angela up when she was crying because it would spoil her. I remember I woke up one day, and I was nervous because I was late feeding her, and then I realized that I hadn't heard her cry. When I got to the room, Angela was just lying there, looking around. I had a sinking feeling that my baby was already getting used to the idea that she could be in need and crying out all she wants, but nobody would be coming and she shouldn't expect it.

I never breastfed any of my children. Joey stayed at the hospital a couple of months because he was so small. When he came home, I attempted to breastfeed him, but he refused because he'd already gotten used to the formula. My family members were disciplinarians who believed in spanking children. Consequently, I spanked my children.

My life as a young mother, even with that "Mrs." in front of my name, was marked by chronic stress. It began to have an adverse effect on my health. I've always tended to be slim, but there came a point when I wasn't holding food down and I lost an alarming amount of weight. My clothes size went down to a five. Now, in the world of Hollywood, that might be cause for a woman to celebrate. But I was diagnosed with a bleeding ulcer—and Hollywood was not even a remote thought. The doctor gave shots in hopes that it would help me properly digest my food, get some nutrients in, and not throw up and cause further damage to my stomach.

One of the straws that broke the camel's back in my marriage to Buddy was not something he did to me but to my mother. Aunt Vera, my mother's sister, had confided in us that my mother had cancer and had been driving herself back and forth to the hospital for treatments. The doctors had told her two years prior that she only had a year to live, but Mother had lived two. My aunt felt that Mother's time to leave was drawing near, so she thought it best to tell us. To make things even worse, my mother was having financial problems and losing her home. One day she dropped by our house for a visit. She was feeling bad and came by so her grandkids could cheer her up. I heard the doorbell ring, and Buddy went to answer it, but when he came back, nobody was with him. "Who was that?" I asked.

He said, "Your mother," and kept walking. He had left her standing at the front door.

When I got to the door, she was already in her car, backing out of the driveway. I could see she was crying. I called her but couldn't get to her, so then I called Aunt Vera. I called Mother all day, until finally she called me and said, "I'm all right." I was livid. Over the years my mother had gone out of her way to help Buddy with many things, and he was rude to her at a time when she was at her lowest. She deserved better.

There was a man named Wingate whom Mother helped get released from jail when he was arrested for running the numbers. I was hoping he'd return the favor and lend her a hand when ownership of her property was threatened, but he didn't. Neither did she find support from Prophet Jones, the popular religious leader in Detroit she had served so well as an aide that he'd titled her "Princess." Maybe he didn't appreciate that when she broke away from him—people charged him with running a cult—she started her own church. She was a preacher who was also clairvoyant, and people would be in line for two hours sometimes to get her counseling. One time a housekeeper brought her white boss, who was a doctor, to talk to her. His daughter was in a coma, and he was heartbroken. Mother told him she would wake up and talk to him, but then after, his daughter would die. And that's exactly what happened. He and most of those she helped turned their backs on her in her time of need. It was almost as if they were happy to see this independent woman go down.

My mother was ever resilient, and even in her sickness, she managed to turn things around.

She found a small building to hold her church services in, lived above it, and made it beautiful. She was known for how she could make everything look so good. Her finances got better around this time too.

She became a minister, with her own religious radio show on WGPR. And parlayed that into good business by selling airtime to other churches to promote their events and their messages. WGPR became very prominent in Detroit because of her.

Mother was a go-getter, a trailblazer, unused to sickness slowing her down. A savvy businessperson in a time when that was not seen as a natural and proper thing for a woman to be, my mother had a record of achievement impressive to anybody paying attention.

Times were tumultuous in America in the 1960s, not just in my family and homelife. But I made the best of the situation.

Dr. King's killing in 1968 caused the Black community to emotionally explode from the volatile mix of grief and anger. They flooded the streets with emotion and sought to draw out and drown out everyone and everything complicit in his assassination. They were met with more guardsmen, more militias, to quell the violence and enforce the curfews. The same troops I navigated through on my way to take food from my mother's church to sell to my coworkers on the job, something I often did. I had errands to run before I could get back home.

Not long after the riots broke out in Detroit, Mother's health took a turn for the worse. The breast cancer she had overtook her. She was such a strong woman, and despite the years of separation from me, from us, the idea that she would never be there for us again was unthinkable. Even at her lowest, the moments when her world seemed to crumble, her determination and faith carried her through. Not this time. She would transition at age fifty-five, the same age that my father had, twenty years before.

On my last visit with her, she was in the hospital, and the doctor was in the room chatting with my mother, and he said she could go home Monday because she was getting better. Mother looked at me and said, "Call Alfreda [that was her seamstress] and tell her to have my dress ready for Sunday." The doctor looked at me and shook his head, telling me not to pay attention to her.

Again, Mother told me, "Don't pay any attention to him. Call Alfreda." The dress she wanted from Alfreda was for her funeral. Mother knew she was dying. She left on that Sunday in 1967, just like she said.

The doctor was in shock, and so were we.

On the day she died, my sister Frieda was headed to pick me up so we could visit Mother at the hospital. It was the one time Frieda was late. My sister was always prompt. For the life of me, I couldn't figure out where she was. Turns out, she had gotten tied up talking to a friend. We finally arrived at the hospital, and as we were walking down the corridor toward her room, the doctor approached us and started explaining that she had expired. Frieda said, "You mean she's dead?"

Mother didn't wait for us to get there, or maybe we weren't supposed to be there. The nurse told us that just before our arrival, she'd been sitting up in bed and said to the nurse, "You're so nice."

The nurse replied, "You're nice to be nice too."

Next, Mother requested a glass of water, and the nurse said that as she started to leave the room, she heard the death rattle. She turned around, and just like that, Mother was gone.

Losing her was overwhelming. Often with situations like the death of a family member, I don't feel things right away. It was like I was in a vacuum. Plus, we were so busy after her death, making arrangements and tying up loose ends with her business, that the emotions didn't have time to take over. Mother put a lot of her own money into her church and took care of the salaries. Now the church was making money, so Mother had made me sit down with her to decide which accounts to withdraw from so she could recoup some of her money. I feel like Mother was really making sure she could pay for her funeral expenses as well as give each of us something.

She was friends with the owner of a mortuary, who was also a member of her church. She'd made previous arrangements with him for the kind of casket she wanted. She already had the funeral planned and even told me how much we should pay for the casket. The mortuary owner kept pressing me to find out how much money she'd left. I told him the casket she'd picked out and the price she had been quoted. He was carrying on like we had to purchase another casket because the one she'd picked out was not available. With that, I decided to go to another mortuary. Then a white guy walked in and whispered something to the mortuary owner. No one said anything to me, but they rolled out with the casket. It was lavender with angels on the end . . . everything she had described. They'd had the casket all along but were trying to find out how much Mother left so they could increase their price. I was adamant that I would only pay the price she'd been quoted.

Then there was another friend, who sold bootleg clothes, and my mother had loaned her money. She told me to call her and collect it when she passed. I went to the woman to get the money, and she told me, "I owe it to Ophelia. Ophelia is not here anymore." Settling Mother's estate was proving to be very difficult.

But when my mother died, there were at least two thousand cars in the funeral procession. And *Jet* magazine reported that more than three thousand people attended her funeral. Princess Ophelia, once a teenage mom rejected by the very people who should have loved her, grew to become a leader, an inspiration, and a pillar of the community among women and men.

Seeing my struggles in the last years of her life, my mother suggested that I get away from Buddy, from the children, and from Detroit. My sister Frieda was living in Los Angeles, so I went there. I took Mother's advice. Frieda had gotten into the movie business as a background performer, also known as an extra. Extras didn't have significant speaking parts.

She was an independent woman living a nice life—enough to be regarded back home in Detroit as a local girl who'd made it good. The Black newspapers would announce her arrival to town when she visited.

We would get so excited whenever we saw her on TV, and now I was where it was all happening.

Los Angeles was something different from the cities in the Midwest. Unlike Chicago and Detroit, the city had palm trees, warm weather, and clean streets. There was no snow to shovel in the winter. You didn't worry about the necessity of socks and shoes that could protect you from frostbite.

In addition to better weather and pretty scenery, there was a lot of progress going on. Black people were taking advantage of opportunities they might not have had back East and down South. They were, for example, buying apartment buildings. I saw that and suggested to my mother that she could do well out here. I was ready to try new things and decided on a whim to take an acting class with Lillian Randolph, a well-known Black actress, and a ballet class. I continued to work for United Airlines. I had been working as a reservationist for United Airlines and was able to transfer my position to LA. And I took on an additional job at the Bank of America on Western Avenue and Washington Boulevard.

After some time had passed and I began to think about returning to the Midwest, the manager of the Bank of America offered to give me a double raise if I stayed in LA for around eight or nine months before going back home. It was enough time for me to know that I wanted to come back. I enjoyed myself over the eight, nine months I stayed in Los Angeles and could see myself living there.

The break from Detroit was good to me, except for the separation from my children. I missed them terribly, and things were not going as well back home as I had hoped. I discovered that the babysitters Buddy hired to help him were sometimes abusive to our children. One of them pressed a fork to Angela's neck. Buddy was neither making sure that they treated the children well nor treating them well himself.

He was dumping his responsibility as a parent onto Angela especially. He had behaved like a loving and attentive father to Angela when she was small. But that had changed. He expected her to play the role of the woman of the house and acted like she was a grown woman, as if he forgot that she was still a young girl. He was leaving it to her to care for and feed her little brothers, especially our youngest child, Dorian.

Jordan had basketball and other sports activities to distract him from the problems at home. But this was not an easy time for him either. He recalled how his father failed to notice when the Detroit cold seeped through the holes in the bottoms of his shoes. Sure, there were some good things. Buddy could delight the children, encouraging them to enjoy board games, such as Monopoly, and card games, including Tonk and blackjack. He'd let them gamble small amounts of money too. But knowing how to appreciate the good side while facing the bad was a tall order—it still is.

As a father and husband, Buddy could be fun and thoughtful one day and irresponsible the next. One of our best family memories with him was when he brought home a puppy we named Cato. Buddy brought us a puppy, but he beat him too. From the time Angela was five or six years old, she witnessed me being assaulted by the only father that she'd ever known.

My son Jordan, who otherwise idolized his dad, was traumatized as well by seeing Buddy bully and hit on me. We were all a bit afraid of how the man of the house would show up from one day to the next. Like most people, including abusers, Buddy had a good side to his personality and a frightening side as well. Dorian, the baby of the family, was probably doing better than any of us with his big sister looking after him. He spent his adorable self running around the house with a towel tied around his neck, playing the superhero. He was the least aware of the trouble swirling around him.

What I did pick up on first was a personality change in my daughter. She had usually been a vibrant, energetic child, but now she was sounding disturbingly different when we talked on the phone. I could tell that she was trying to put on a brave face for me. She was protective of me by nature and didn't want to tell me what was really going on. Not even a teenager yet, she was already trying to look after everyone. I ache when I think about it. I ended up leaving Los Angeles knowing that I would get the children and our belongings, and soon return to LA with them.

Once Mother passed away, there was nothing nor anyone to keep me in Detroit. I started plotting my final escape to the West Coast. I began to accumulate and hide the things the children and I would need to resettle. We had a small storage area in the basement that we never used and Buddy never went into. My intention wasn't to take much from the home we'd made together. I especially intended to leave Buddy with anything he had paid a dime on because I didn't want any trouble out of him. He could have the living room set, our bedroom set, the washer, the dryer, the stove, and the refrigerator as far as I was concerned. I thought that if I left the household intact, it would be easy for him and his girlfriend to carry on, and he would leave me in peace.

The children and I had suitcases hidden under the bed, and it was important that everything went as planned, or I would once again face an angry and likely violent Buddy. On this day I packed up my station wagon and my three kids, along with our dog, Cato, and left for good. Earlier that morning I called my husband while he was at work to find out when he'd be home. He would usually go to the bowling alley or bar after work, and I was counting on it. Much to my dismay, he said he was heading straight home. I did my best not to panic, but I knew we needed to move fast. I told the kids what to pack and what to leave. We only had four hours to get our belongings and get out of Dodge. I had already convinced Bekins Moving Company to allow me to bring my furniture to them instead of having them pick it up and load it. A family friend who owned a truck agreed to take my furniture to Bekins the morning we were leaving in exchange for my station wagon. This way our neighbors would have no idea that I'd left. I wanted my soon-to-be ex-husband to think we were still in Detroit.

Like so many women of my generation, I held on to an abusive husband for too long. I did it for the sake of our kids and for the idea that marriage is until death do you part. But I realized, if there was going to be a death, it was likely going to be mine. So it was time to go. There was nothing left for me to hold on to, and the idea that this broken marriage was good for raising our children had been long disproven. Let the girlfriend have her turn.

This change, this uprooting ourselves to go to a new and mostly unfamiliar place, would and did have a big impact on all of us. We had been fortunate in Detroit to live in a neighborhood where the kids enjoyed their days relatively safe. Jordan was occupied with basketball and other sports. He was a good son and a loving brother to Dorian and his big sister, Angela.

Just as Angela took responsibility for and looked after her younger brothers, she was a leader among the children in the community as well. She was a peacemaker, a comforter. Her Spirit had been bruised by the abuse that she'd experienced, but she was resilient, strong, and enormously creative.

When the time came for us to leave, Jordan was the least among us ready to go. He had visited his aunt in Los Angeles before, including on a trip to Disneyland, and loved it. But it isn't easy leaving what is familiar to you, even if it is far from perfect.

I had moments of hesitation as well, because I thought it was wrong to leave Buddy with my bills, so my idea was to pay them off and then leave. One day Angela and Jordan came to me and asked, "How much do you owe?" It was a moment of clarity for me. All this time, I thought I was staying there for their happiness; it was then I realized that, like me, they were ready to go. They were tired of seeing me beaten by him.

Nonetheless, Los Angeles was a place of new possibilities for us. But in the words of Langston Hughes, there would be no "crystal stair" awaiting the children and me.

Our struggles would not end, but an altogether better life could begin.

While staying with my sister Frieda, I'd found a small but quaint place on Crenshaw and Olympic Boulevards to rent. It had been converted to an office, so the kids and I took pleasure in converting it back to a home for us. We painted it, and it was really cute. Joey and Dorian shared a bedroom, while Angela, who was a teen by this time, had her own room, and I had mine. California turned out to be an ideal place for me—even as a single mother. To show you how God laid everything out: I would take the bus on Crenshaw Boulevard and go north to Wilshire Boulevard, where the bus dropped me right across from United Airlines. My son Joey would take the bus to the left on Wilshire to John Burroughs Middle School. Dorian would walk over a block to school, and Angela would go on a few blocks over to Olympic, to Los Angeles High School. Across the street was Boy's Supermarket. I didn't need a car. We could go grocery shopping and take the cart to our house. Everything was laid out perfectly.

I did call Buddy. He couldn't trace my location from the phone number. I couldn't forbid my children from talking to their father, but every time Buddy talked to our Joey on the phone, Joey would cry, and I would feel terrible. Then something so tragic—unspeakable, really—happened to Joey. I was at work, and he and Angela were at my sister's home.

He went down to the corner to buy some candy, and this guy approached him. "You want a job?"

Joey said, "Yeah." He was so excited because he wanted to work. He ran back to the house and told Angela, "This guy said he's going to take me down to Sears. They're hiring."

The guy took him across from the Sears and told him the trucks parked in the back, and then he held Joey at knifepoint while he sexually assaulted him. The guy was sixteen years old but looked older and had a much bigger build. The police called me at work, and I left to get Joey. My sister, who had also spoken to the police, told me that they'd suggested that we not talk to Joey about what had happened to him or touch him. I regret that I took their advice and didn't do what came natural to me: to hug and comfort him. We knew so little about how to deal with these traumas back then. In hindsight, I should have followed my instinct to hold Joey tight.

The sixteen-year-old was arrested and charged. I was by Joey's side in court when we learned that the perpetrator had molested at least thirteen children. They were all there in the courtroom. We also found out that the guy had confessed. The perpetrator's mother was there too, and she was devastated. I felt sorry for her. When I found out she had no transportation home, I offered her a ride. She told me she had taken her son from her husband and had moved to Los Angeles, and her son had never forgiven her. She said her sister kept telling her, "Something is wrong with him." But she wouldn't believe it. She was heartbroken. It was then that I wondered if Joey was having problems because I'd taken him from his father. Giving her a ride that day with my son—her son's victim—in the car might have been a terrible idea. I didn't consider enough what that decision did to Joey. Did I add to his trauma? All I am sure about now is that I can't take that decision back. I can only live for, learn about, and love my son as best I can.

But the nightmare didn't stop there. This time in my life, I can truly say, was the dark night of my soul. I wish I could say I left my abusive husband, came to LA, and started my career. But the truth is, I had some tough mountains to climb. I made the same mistake a lot of women make. Not only was my son molested, but I would soon learn that my daughter was also molested—not by a stranger, but by Buddy, my husband. The man I had grown up with since I was nine years old. I could not believe he had become that monster. To add insult to injury, my mother had predicted that he would get in bed with Angela, and I hadn't believed it. It was during the time my mother was dying and I was spending lots of time at the hospital that Buddy chose to do it. Angela was thirteen. Buddy had come home after a night of drinking and gotten into bed with Angela. He had already molested her on the piano bench. She'd been on high alert since then and later told me she heard a whisper earlier that day as he walked by her: "He's going to get in bed with you tonight." Angela didn't tell me until long after we were gone. She was afraid of him, and because I was unprotected, she felt she was too. My poor daughter described how she made efforts to avoid his awful behavior. After all of this, I still went back to him. It is hard to share this story, but I feel that someone out there may benefit from hearing the truth. We make mistakes, but we can overcome them.

Mothers should listen to their daughters and sons, and let them know they believe them and support them. If not, it sends a message to them that what happened was their fault and that they are not worthy of protection. That it's okay to accept the unacceptable. Angela struggled a lot, as did my son, as they tried to find their way back to knowing their worth. With my son it was clear what happened because the perpetrator was a stranger, but it was too hard to wrap my head around what had happened to my daughter for years. Today she finally knows that I believe her, and it has made all the difference in our relationship and in our individual lives.

The story of how I ended up back with Buddy goes like this: My girlfriend Marion, whom I traded places with at United Airlines, had a husband whose job transferred him around the country. When he was asked to move back to Detroit, she and I were able to make that trade. When they returned to Detroit, they threw a party. Obviously, there was some talk about Marion being able to trade with me, because one of their guests ran into my husband later at a bar and said, "Man, your wife is in California." Marion was also a friend who grew up with Frieda.

She would never have told Buddy where I was, but someone at that party had loose lips. When Buddy found out, he began scheming on a plan. He went to his ex-wife and asked if he could take their youngest daughter, Gisele, to Chicago to meet his mother. Which they did; however, Buddy also brought her to California without permission, hoping that I would let them in when I saw that Gisele was with him.

A neighbor whom I had confided in about the move called me and said that the day we left, when Buddy came home from work . . . he came running out in the street, yelling, "My family. Where's my family? My family is gone!"

My aunt would call me and say, "I feel sorry for Buddy."

I said, "You better not tell him where I am. Just feel sorry, because you weren't feeling sorry for me when he was beating my ass and acting crazy." To protect where I was, I informed my coworkers that if Buddy called, they should tell him I had quit and they didn't know where I was.

Frieda called me one day and said, "I hate to tell you this, but Buddy is standing in my living room."

I said, "Well, you might as well send him here, because he's going to be at United Airlines next." Buddy brought his daughter and told me he wanted to come back. I said, "I do not love you. But if you would be a father to the children, we can be friends and then see if anything else develops."

I figured, since he had driven all the way to California and didn't know anyone, I would relent. Plus, I thought the children needed their father, especially Joey. *I might as well go on and give it one more try*, I decided. But this was without considering what my daughter had been through.

We bought a house on Sierra Bonita Avenue. It was such a nice house, and I loved fixing it up. The master bedroom had an extra room added to it, which I made a den. Buddy kept insisting that he wanted to be my husband and things would be different. I prayed that this time things would work out.

CHAPTER FOUR

Theater Saved My Life

Acting saved me at a time in my life when I was broken. . . . I grew by connecting with the emotions of a character.

Angela was taking drama classes in high school, and she loved them. I thought that I'd like them too and certainly thought they were a great activity for us to do together—and they were affordable. I found out about an organization called the Performing Arts Society of Los Angeles (PASLA) that could help us. Los Angeles in general and our neighborhood specifically were known for producing and attracting artists. And many were also activists who regarded their work as a way to not only enhance their individual lives but to advance the Black and poor communities of Los Angeles politically, culturally, and economically.

The uprisings in Los Angeles during the 1960s, particularly in 1965, unified and energized a generation of young Black people. In August of that year, thousands of Black youth rose up in protest in Watts. While many people look back on those times with regret, there were some good outcomes for the Black community. The problems of gang conflicts were reduced if not solved for a number of years after, and the Watts Renaissance, the city's most important arts and literary movement of the decade, was born. My family, the community, and I benefited from that in many ways. I discovered acting was a way to become the person I wanted to be. And I would soon be on a career-making and history-making show on the nation's most popular form of entertainment at the time: television.

We joined an acting workshop held by PASLA. We only had to pay three dollars for our clipboard, and that was the cost. The workshop was in a black box with a small stage, but to us it was the real deal. It was magical. We were so excited. I remember one night, when everyone had gone, Angela and I went and stood on the stage, mesmerized.

We studied acting together as an inexpensive way to share activities and bond. But it was Angela, before me, who began to get hired to work in front of the camera in film and television, including the movie *Cleopatra Jones* and the television show *Sanford and Son*. I got ideas for what was possible for me when visiting her on sets with her own dressing room and trailer. She was experiencing professional success, but also the hazards of a career in show business on and off the set. She found herself in ugly situations and, like Jordan, was sexually assaulted. In her case, she was set up by another young woman to be taken advantage of at a nightclub. Then again, a trusted colleague, or so we thought, set her up with some older man. Fortunately, having learned a hard lesson from before, she successfully talked the setup guy into taking her home and not leaving her alone with and at the mercy of her would-be attacker.

This was a time when Black Americans were individually and collectively pursuing more information about our African past and identifying more with its cultures, including its names. The founder and director of PASLA was Motojicho, aka Vantile Whitfield. Our first instructor was a man named Dhahabu, aka Lucien Smith. Another teacher was Jitahadi, aka Nathaniel Taylor. He became known for his role as Rollo on *Sanford and Son* and later guest-starred on *227*. The workshop was full of aspiring and professional actors. But not everyone went on to pursue a career in acting. Nonetheless, the talent was abundant, and we fed off each other. I met two lifelong friends there, Della Thomas and Judelle Turner-Moore. Ta-Tanisha, who was one of the stars of *Room 222*, had gone there, along with her husband, Lee Weaver, who was also an esteemed actor. Years later I would bring Lee on *227* as the original mailman. Barbara O. Jones was also a member of the workshop. She became famous for her standout role in the groundbreaking film *Daughters of the Dust* by Julie Dash.

People think my daughter followed me into the business, but I actually followed her. She moved on from *Cleopatra Jones* to *Sanford and Son*, and then she starred in her first movie, *The Young Nurses*. She was a nurse who was being chased by some bad guys. Angela lied and said she could ride a motorcycle at the urging of her agent. Turns out she had to ride the whole movie, and of course she had never been on one. The chase scenes are hysterical, because the music is so intense, but it looks like Angela and the car that's chasing her are going five miles per hour.

Theater for both of us was a great teacher and gave us the best foundation. In fact, theater was fast becoming my first true love. I could take on characters and get out of myself, which for me was really good because I was so insecure. I never thought I'd ever make it as an actress. To be honest, it seemed like I couldn't even get my life together. Back then my confidence level was about as high as the gutter. And that would be reinforced later when Buddy attended the plays Angela and I did and was asked what he thought of my performance. Buddy would ignore the question and instead answer, "Angela was good." He could never compliment me. He'd rather have given me a black eye. He acted jealous of any good thing that came my way. Thankfully many others thought I had talent and encouraged me.

Vantile left PASLA to run the Washington, DC–based National Endowment for the Arts. It was right around the time that our class graduated to the advanced level of PASLA's acting courses. Vantile's move out East motivated us to follow Roger Mosley, who was also in our workshop, over to Mafundi Institute in Watts, where Raymond St. Jacques was the instructor, followed by Nina Foch. We also heard that casting for a production of *Native Son* by Richard Wright was going on down the street at the Watts Writers Workshop. Roger was cast as Bigger, the central character in Wright's story. I was his mother, and Angela was his sister. We had a meager budget, as with most theater productions at the time, and so I took on the task of making a fake rat. I got a dark gray sock and electrical tape for the tail, and used pipe cleaners to hold it together. Angela sat there the whole time I was making the rat until I got close to the end; suddenly she jumped up and ran and locked herself in the bathroom. I called after her, "Angela, you saw me make it. You know it's not real." But she would not come out. We still laugh about that. I guess I did a great job. The next play we did was called *A Play For, By, and About Black People*. It was a series of vignettes we created from the workshop that Roger Mosley was now heading. The esteemed actor/producer Max Julien (who was popular for movies like *The Mack*) came to see the play and picked Angela to be in his movie *Cleopatra Jones*.

That's what started her career, got her in the union, and found her an agent.

While she was doing that, I was cast in a blaxploitation movie, *Sweet Jesus, Preacherman*, which was released in 1973. I played Beverly Solomon, a member of a Baptist church where a gangster was posing as the preacher.

We were busy. Our hobby—the medicine for our bruised Spirits—was becoming a lifestyle. *Happy Days* was our next play, and it turned out to be my favorite, because it was a story about life in the hood. We opened with Barbra Streisand singing her song "Happy Days Are Here Again." We worked as both actors and crew. We didn't have a lot of money, so believe it or not, we built our set out of Styrofoam, and it looked good. We even made a casket out of the stuff, and it looked so good that somebody stole it. After it was lifted, we had enough left in our budget to build half a casket, and we put a weight inside of it so it wouldn't fall over. It was fragile. Now, the rule was, no matter what, DO NOT TOUCH THE SET.

Every day Roger would remind us not to touch it. My friend Della played a neighbor in the production who comes over and gets me drunk. One night I was really riding the wave of the moment. I felt drunk and decided to stumble across the stage and lean on the wall . . . but of course, it wasn't a wall, it was Styrofoam! So down the set went, all around us. The audience was laughing so hard, but I knew I was in trouble, so I kept on going and said, "That's why we need to get out of the hood. The whole place is falling apart." Roger did not find any of this funny.

Angela and I had a scene at the end of the play where she comes in, angry, to tell me that my child is in the morgue. I was supposed to cry, but for some reason, her mouth looked contorted every time she said "morgue," and it cracked me up, but since my back was to the audience, they couldn't see me laughing—but they could see Angela, who had a look of horror on her face. This got her even more upset, which made me laugh harder.

Another night we were in the middle of the funeral scene, and we got so riled up from the preacher's eulogy that a few cast members started stomping their feet, and of course, the half casket fell over. I had to sit the casket back up and hold on to it. We had to hide our faces so the audience wouldn't see us laugh. I loved that play most of all.

The idea of me working part-time to become an actor—raising three children on one income—was ridiculous and irresponsible to my child-free sister. And furthermore, she believed the community theater I was doing would lead to a dead end. It's an opinion that many people, in and out of the industry, would have had about me then, and a belief that has held many women of a certain age, with and without children, back, especially if they are also Black.

While the family was thrilled to see Frieda in any role

possible on TV, my sister was not as thrilled for me when she heard me talking about giving acting a try. I had hoped this was something we could pursue together, but Frieda was not happy. She'd wanted me to move to California, even encouraged me, but she wasn't necessarily planning for me to get into show business like her. Later, once I started doing plays, she said, "What do you think you're going to do with this? Pretty girls have a hard time making it in Hollywood, so what are you going to do?"

My personal life was even less encouraging than Frieda was. As a way of helping my son, I'd invited Buddy back into our household and fully again into our lives. This turn of events that I thought might help my son at the same time boded terribly for my daughter. The idea that she would live again under the same roof as her abuser was unacceptable.

Buddy had gone back to his old ways, and I knew I had to end the marriage for good. Otherwise, he was not going to let me have an acting career. I knew there would come a day when I needed to be onstage, and he would hurt me so I couldn't go. I didn't know how I was going to leave, and then the day came when the choice was made for me. One night he tried to sodomize me, but I wasn't having it. We started to fight and fell over on the floor. Buddy straddled me and was going to beat my face, but I grabbed him by his hair and held him close to me so he couldn't hit me. He was on top of me but couldn't get free. Suddenly Angela ran in the room and screamed at him, "Let her go!" Buddy was trying to tell her that he wasn't holding me, I was holding him, but Angela didn't hear him. She hit him in the head with a bottle several times until it broke. We had three steps from our bedroom that led down to the den. Buddy fell down the steps, dazed, but to our surprise, he regained his balance and got up. So, I yelled, "Run, Angela!" She ran across the street to the neighbors. I tried to run into the bathroom, but he came in after me. My sons were trying to help me, but to my horror, Dorian, who was the smallest at the time, came in with a bat. Buddy snatched it and came in after me. He didn't hit me with the bat, but he threatened me.

He said, "Go get Angela and bring her back."

I played along. "Okay, okay, I'll go."

As soon as I got out of the door and yelled "Call the police," Buddy drove off, and when he came back, the police were still there. They asked me if I wanted to file a complaint, and I said yes.

"What are you doing?" Buddy asked.

I looked him in the eye and said firmly, "I'm filing a complaint against you!" I knew I couldn't let him stay; he had threatened to hurt Angela when she came back to the house. I signed the complaint, and they took him to jail. The next day was the Fourth of July, and I had planned a barbeque because my mother's sister, my aunt Vera, was visiting from Detroit, along with a couple of other family members.

During the afternoon Dorian ran into the house in a panic. "Daddy's coming down the street!"

I thought they would have at least kept him in jail over the holiday. Buddy came in, and I said sweetly, "Are you hungry? You want something to eat?"

He said, "You know what you told me about Angela's father? I think that was me too. I was on drugs." He was clearly making an excuse for his behavior.

I just said, "Oh, okay." I took Buddy his plate, and while I was laughing and talking to family, I was also packing and carrying my belongings out to the car.

Joey came to me and said, "Why don't you and Angela go? Dorian and I will be all right."

So when the party was done, I came into the house and said, "See y'all," and Angela and I drove off. I hated to leave Aunt Vera, and I especially did not want to leave my sons. All I knew was that we could not go back, only forward. I prayed that God would show me the way. Later Joey told me that Buddy had laid a gun on the bed and told the boys that it was for Angela.

For a while my friend Della let us sleep on her sofa. My youngest son, Dorian, has always had a great sense of direction. You take him to a place one time, and he can take you right back there. I had let Dorian come visit, and Buddy found out. He made Dorian get in the car and show him where I was. Angela ran in and said, "Daddy's out there."

I'd just bought a new car, and Buddy must have been spying on me, because later, when I got in my car, he started chasing me. I made it to Adams Boulevard and saw that the right-turn lane was tight. I didn't have much space, but I managed to squeeze through. Buddy wasn't as lucky and damaged his car trying to follow me. This made him livid. I kept going and was nearing La Brea. I could see that Buddy was closing in on me again. There was a red light in front of me, and I knew I was trapped. I crossed over to the left and swung into a gas station. The men standing in the station were running for dear life. Buddy followed me and smashed into my car. Buddy got out and was standing to the left of me, banging on the door and demanding I open it. I pretended to cry and turned my face to the left, where a man was standing. I mouthed to him, "Call the police," so that Buddy couldn't see. Thank God, he called them.

When the police arrived, Buddy was suddenly sane and speaking very nicely. He later said one of the men asked him, "Isn't that your wife? Don't you love her?"

I got out of the car and told the police, "This man and I are divorced. He needs to pay for my damages, and please don't let him follow me." They made Buddy admit he was at fault, and that was the last time he followed me.

· Act One ·
The Days Before Stardom

This is one of the headshots I took before I started working as an actress. People love this photo, and I think it's because of the Afro. It was before the world knew my face. I'm just glad I didn't look like all I'd been through.

This is my mother on the right sitting in her parlor with her brother, Harry, in the middle and her sister Vera on the left.

This is my dad, Douglas, who I grew up with and loved so much. We really had a special connection. Everyone called him Bootsie. He died in 1947 when I was sixteen.

I was named after my aunt Margaret, my mother's older sister. Margaret had to give up her childhood to raise my mother and Aunt Vera after their mother died.

This is my mother, Ophelia Kemp, in her first home in Detroit. She was once named the best-dressed woman in Detroit.

This is my older sister, Vera Louise—who I grew up with in Chicago—on the day she married Claiborne James Robinson. Vera Louise was a Leo and always had a lion's personality. She went for what she wanted.

In my day, we didn't really have weaves, but we had falls. This is me and my first fall. Finally, I had long hair. Later I would learn to love my natural hair.

Standing at the back: Me, pregnant there with Joey; my ex-husband, Buddy; my sister's nieces Gloria Jean and Etherine; my older sister Vera Louise, my sister Freida, then my mother, Ophelia, on the far right. *Seated:* Below my mother is Basil, their daughter Bernadette, and my mother's sister Vera, and next to her is my grandfather and his wife. *Front:* The children in the front are twins Gerald and Phillip; Jesse Kemp; my baby girl, Angela; and Louise's son, Russel.

This is my daughter, Angela, sitting in my mother's parlor underneath the painting of my sister Frieda, who along with being a model also studied ballet.

Working for United enabled me to take the children on summer vacations. Here we are visiting Washington, DC, when Angela was thirteen, Joey was eleven, and Dorian was four. We went to a museum and then the zoo, where Joey poked the cheetah through the fence. We were lucky that day. Joey was fine, but the security guard was not happy.

• Act Two •
Hello, Hollywood

Lil Cumber (my first agent) had me take photos like these as a maid for my headshots. I didn't want to take those pictures, but they ended up getting me the audition for *The Jeffersons*.

Natalie Cole and I became friends after we shot the film *Lily in Winter*. I threw my grandson a surprise party and Natalie brought her son, Robby. Robby and Amil always talked about how much they enjoyed that party . . . may they both rest in peace.

The people who brought *The Jeffersons* and *227* to life onscreen with me (like Hal Williams here on the right) remain in my heart. And staying close with Lenny Kravitz has been one way of keeping the memory of my friend and his mother, Roxie Roker, (seen here in the framed photo) alive as well.

I was on the cover of *Jet* magazine to promote my new show *227*. When I was growing up, being on the cover of *Jet* was a big deal in the Black community, so I was really proud that I made the cover.

This was when I was asked to host *The Late Show*. They were looking for someone to replace Joan Rivers, so I got a shot. I was nervous but ended up having a great time. Roxie Roker and Franklin Cover were two of my guests.

I really could never thank Oprah enough for writing that check to help me try to save the building and preserve my vision for the community.

· Act Three ·
Community, Family & Purpose

Singing at my club with my dear friend the late Gerald Wiggins. "Wig" was a renowned jazz pianist band leader.

My kids, Angela, Jordan, and Dorian, all sang at the club and opened for me. They said it was a dream come true. We had a ball.

My daughter's wedding day. She was a beautiful bride. Although the marriage didn't last, it was meaningful in that her husband moved them to Atlanta, and in some ways, we believe saved my grandson.

My grandson Amil graduating from eighth grade. He attended Pilgrim Junior High and here he was on the way to Hamilton High.

I was so glad that I got to work with Betty White on *Hot in Cleveland*. My fellow octogenarian definitely understood my mantra that it's never too late.

Nothing can break the bond I have with my onscreen daughter, Regina. We're family.

Muhammad Ali would come to the club and do magic for my grandson and the other children. I really liked him. He loved to play jokes on me. He was very funny and very kind. The greatest.

It's such a joy to be able to stop by and check out my star on the Hollywood Walk of Fame. Receiving that honor in 2021 was one of the highlights of my career.

CHAPTER FIVE

The Cost of Love and Silence

All my kids had to learn to keep secrets. That's what you put on them when they grow up in an unsafe home.

My daughter and I did some background work in a couple of films, one of which was *Lady Sings the Blues*, starring Diana Ross and Billy Dee Williams. We sat in the club scene and watched Diana Ross do take after flawless take. The experience affirmed what we already knew: Acting was the kind of work we wanted to do. Somebody had advised us not to do too much background work—the kind of acting work my sister Frieda did. They were of the opinion that the pay was not great and that taking those kinds of jobs wasn't what we should do "if we were serious about acting." So when the casting agent for *Lady Sings the Blues* called us again, we declined. "No thank you," I said. When asked why, I replied, "Because we want to do what Diana Ross is doing."

They said, "Well, good luck. We all want to do that."

I said, "Yeah, but we're going to do it."

My friend Della, another aspiring actor, and I were bold. We would go onto studio lots and say, "Hello, we're actresses, and we have our résumés." Most times we weren't allowed into the offices. But one time we struck gold.

Casting director and producer Joyce Selznick was in her office on the lot and said, "Come on in, girls." Joyce was the niece of David O. Selznick, known for classics like *Gone with the Wind*. He was also once the head of 20th Century Fox. We told her we were actresses, and she corrected us and said, "No, you're students." Joyce laid it out for us and gave us twenty minutes of her time, explaining the business of Hollywood and how to navigate it. I'll always appreciate her for that.

One day Della and I were at the DMV on Cole Avenue. We heard there was a film project across the street, and they were looking for actors. Della and I made our way over there and introduced ourselves. We told them about our workshop at Mafundi. To our surprise, the producers came to see us! They ended up casting Roger Mosley as the lead of the film *Sweet Jesus, Preacherman*. I was cast as his girlfriend. Della was given a role, and in fact, half the workshop got to work in the film.

I needed an agent. So I went to meet the one who represented my sister Frieda. Her name was Lillian Cumber, the only Black female agent on the West Coast at that time. This was of course a time when Hollywood wasn't widely accepting of Black actors. We had a hard time landing roles and signing with people who could support us in finding those roles. There was Lillian Cumber on the West Coast and Ernestine McClendon, New York City's first Black theatrical agent, on the East.

Cumber took me on, but she and I didn't always see eye to eye. Actors, for example, need photos, headshots, and such to send around to casting agents. Your agent's job is to help you project an image that fits the available roles, the characters you're meant to play. Lil had me take a photo with a broom in my hand. I didn't like it.

She was in the business because she knew who and what Hollywood wanted from Black people. Lil was selling us as domestics, knowing that would work. I wanted more. All Black artists wanted more. I might have found my own photographer and someone to style the shoot. But her clients were obliged to use her people. I'm pretty sure she made some money from that.

I was new in this business, so I took the photo her way. Shortly thereafter I was cast in *Sweet Jesus, Preacherman.*

I had gotten the film on my own after I'd approached the producers.

Given that Lil was my agent, I needed her to sign the contract. When I asked her as my agent to please come and sign the contract, she refused. "I'm not coming down there," she said. And with an attitude. She was referring to the neighborhood. She was Black, but she was very Hollywood. She wasn't leaving Tinseltown to come down to where *Sweet Jesus, Preacherman* was happening. She was too fancy for that. Lil made me bring the movie contract to her. I was not happy.

Needless to say, after that movie I left her. The next film I got was called *Black Belt Jones*, starring the martial arts master Jim Kelly. I did a cameo in that film. It was at this time I decided I wanted to change my name. "Margaret Gibbs" didn't sound fluid to me; I wanted something that would flow. I came up with "Marla" and liked the rhythm of it. I kept "Gibbs" because that was my children's last name, so "Marla Gibbs" it was. It was also time to get a new agent. So I went to the other Black agent, Ernestine McClendon, Cumbers's East Coast counterpart who was now working on the West Coast too. She was freckle-faced and full of fire. She was an agent and an actor, so she understood actors.

I was landing small roles in local theater productions pretty regularly by then. I joined the Zodiac Theater after hearing that it had won a prestigious drama award. I went to see the play *Does a Tiger Wear a Necktie?* Margaret Avery, who is now my good friend, was phenomenal in that production.

We'd all heard how Clint Eastwood came to the play and, after seeing Margaret, cast her in his film. The first play I was cast in there was *The Amen Corner* by James Baldwin. I played the role of Sister Boxer. That's how I met Ted Lange, which led to him casting me in his production of *Medea. The Gingerbread Lady* was next.

During the run of that show, I heard about a casting for a new television series called *The Jeffersons*. I had been in the office of Norman Lear, the show's creator, before, but the casting director had looked right past me to talk to everybody else. I was invisible. How I ended up in her office again in 1975 was because of Ernestine McClendon.

Unhappy with how Hollywood was treating the actors she represented, she took out a full-page ad in *The Hollywood Reporter*, one of the industry's most influential publications at the time. In the ad, she posted an open letter to the entertainment industry, calling it out for its unfairness. She likened the opportunities offered by the film and TV industry to Black artists as a revolving door: in and out. The letter sparked conversation and controversy. It had an impact. Casting agents did increase their calls to her clients. She led the charge for more inclusion in Hollywood and succeeded.

When it comes to the parent-child relationships, sometimes your child needs to find their own answer. About the time I was starting to perform in the theater more, I offered to take Joey, but he didn't want to come to acting class with Angela and me, so I left him at home a lot. And I didn't know what Buddy was saying to him when he came home from work.

When Joey was a preteen, I bought him a lawn mower and suggested he go around to the neighbors whose yards looked unkempt and offer to mow their lawns for a reasonable price. Joey managed to build his clientele up to three houses, and it did wonders for his self-confidence. When Buddy came back and found out, he told me that his son didn't need to do lawn work for anyone. Instead of him being proud of Joey, Buddy deflated him.

A while later Joey asked me to sign him up for a basketball camp. Here came Buddy again saying he couldn't go, and I saw that it upset Joey. I put my foot down and told him, "You're going to basketball camp; don't worry about it." I put the money together and sent him off to the camp, but as luck would have it, the camp didn't turn out great for him. The basketball player who was running the camp was fooling around with the girls, and drugs were present. Joey complained he didn't get the coaching he thought he was going to get.

When it was time for him to go to high school, I enrolled

Joey in Fairfax High. I found out he was ditching school. I was determined to make sure he stayed in school, so when we moved and he started attending Inglewood High, after I dropped him off, I'd circle back around to make sure he hadn't exited. If he did, he would see me and march right back in there. When Joey received his diploma, I told him it was mine, because I'd earned it with all the effort I put in to keep him on track.

It breaks my heart thinking about the traumas Joey endured. I felt terrible and stressed over him a lot.

Joey started on a downward spiral, and I realized he had been deteriorating right before my eyes. How had I missed it? Before I knew it, someone found him standing in the middle of the street, yelling about how the sun was following him. Another time he wandered into a hotel on Century Boulevard and caused a ruckus. I spoke to the police who were there and asked them to help him. He needed to go to a facility. They told me to come get him or they were taking him to jail. He did eventually get put in jail once. Honestly I was a little relieved, because it gave me time to figure out what to do next. He was sent to a facility, where all they did was administer medication, and Joey walked around like a zombie the whole time he was there. He was given Haldol because they discovered he was suffering from bipolar disorder. Because Joey was grown, the doctors told me nothing. It was a horrible time. I knew that my son was in trouble and needed more help than they were giving him.

I went to a psychic, and she said, "You have to get him out of the country." I didn't know where to send him, but I started researching facilities. I heard about a place in Hawaii, and although it wasn't out of the country, I was hopeful I could find some answers. The people that answered the phone turned me off. They bragged too much about how they ran the facility and came off as authoritative gatekeepers. My Spirit said, *Oh, no!* And so the search continued. God works in mysterious ways and is always right on time. Divine order was in full effect. I typically drove my car, but on this day I was on the bus. Sitting next to me was the answer to my prayers! He recognized me as an actress and then said the magic words: "I take clients with addictive behaviors to Cuernavaca, Mexico." Turns out he was a doctor who was an expert in all types of addiction. He showed me a brochure with pictures of the facility he worked at.

When I saw the brochure, I felt this was the place, but I faced a major obstacle. Joey was an adult and would have to agree. I had previously gotten him help many times before, but he'd never fully cooperated. Joey would check himself out, then go back later and insist on being checked back in. We had to put a plan together to get Joey to go and to stay. Again, God was working. Joey forged one of my checks, but because the bank knew him, they allowed him to get away with it. This was a blessing in disguise, because I insisted they press charges. Fortunately, once he was arrested, we could put a plan in action. The doctor spoke with an attorney, who got the judge to give Joey an ultimatum: "Either go to the facility or go to jail."

Now a new obstacle came: A major earthquake hit Mexico. There was no communication, so this was a test of my faith: Did I send him to Mexico anyway, or did I find another place? My Spirit said, *Send Joey to Mexico.* My aunt Vera was visiting, and Joey had a lot of respect for her. When it was time for him to go to the airport, Joey was upset with me, so he would not ride in my car. Instead he rode with Aunt Vera and the doctor. I rode behind them.

The challenges still were not over. When we got to the airport, Joey went to the pay phone and started talking. Call it mother's intuition, but I said to the doctor, "He ain't talking to nobody." I knew he was stalling.

Next Joey went to the doctor and said, "My mother said she gave you money for me. Give me my money." So the doctor did and then went ahead to check him in.

As we neared the gate, the doctor came to us with a look of frustration and said, "The flight has been canceled." My heart dropped. But he said, "Let's check another airline." He found another flight and checked them in.

Before Joey headed to the plane, he went to the bathroom. I said, "Don't follow him; he's going in there to cry." I knew this all was hard for Joey. Vera and I stayed at the gate to make sure he took off. I didn't want to see those long legs walking back off the plane. Two weeks later I received a telex (they still didn't have any phone service because of the earthquake) saying, "Jordan wants to know if he can stay." That was music to my ears.

Dorian, Angela, and I went to visit Joey. When we got there, we were driven up to these gates. They were tall and foreboding. I thought, *What have I done? Where have I sent my son?* But when the gates opened, we saw this beautiful estate. A mansion, tennis courts, a pool and a cabana, rolling lawns, lush landscapes, and a doctor walking the grounds with a patient. Joey's room was even more breathtaking. It looked like something out of *Better Homes & Gardens*. It featured a shower big enough for four people. Outside of his room was a tea-and-coffee service. I wanted to stay there! There were other patients there for other addictions, such as opioids, sex, and food. Joey received a total of seven hours of counseling per day. The estate had several areas where the patients could receive treatments. They could walk the grounds with their doctors or counselors; they could sit in the cabana or hang in the office or living room. With all of the top-notch treatment he was receiving, I wanted him to stay there for six months at least and learn the language. But he came back after three. Upon returning, he had to go to a halfway house. Sadly, even after all of this, he went back on drugs again. I learned later that I was pouring more into his recovery than he was. Joey needed to be responsible for his own way back.

I'm known as Miss Fix It, which is not always a good thing. If there's a problem, I'm going to chase down a solution. I don't know how not to do that. But that means I'm trying to control things. When Joey finally got clean, he did it himself. I am proud to say he is more than thirty-two years clean and sober, and has written an inspirational book called *Sober Eyes: A Poetic Expression of Life Filled with Alcohol, Drugs, Gambling, Sex, Mental Illness and Recovery from It All.* He is also a successful real estate broker.

Just when I felt I had gotten a handle on parenting, it was time to release Angela and Joey into the world. There was a time when my eldest child, Angela, distanced herself from me. That was very hard for me. She had told me that I was her best friend, and I needed one, so I took her literally. I know now that back then I parentified Angela. She was in charge of helping her brothers with homework, helping me with dinner because I was working, and cleaning the kitchen so that when Buddy came home, he'd have no excuse to fight. And she was always there when we were fighting, trying to protect me. She was hurting too, especially when I took Buddy back after she told me what had happened. But she always looked like she was okay. She was acting with me, and all seemed well. It's the squeaky wheel that gets the oil, and Angela wasn't squeaking. Actually she was, but she was good at hiding it. She was smoking weed, ditching school, sneaking out of the window, and even hitchhiking—and all the while getting good grades, so that of course I didn't know all the other things were going on.

It wasn't until she ran away that Joey told me what had been going on. He was worried about her, and so was I. One day I was so upset that she was gone that I started to cry. Buddy was jealous and slapped me. He would always bring up the fact that Harvey was her father, and Buddy felt she got more attention than he did. It threw me because he had been so attentive to her when she was young. Well, to restate the facts, Buddy was kind to her until she was about five . . . then he changed. When Angela was ready to come back home, I sent her to counseling. I was waiting for the therapist to invite me in, but she never did.

Mothers need to understand that even though we depend on our daughters and they seem mature, we forget that they are still growing and maturing and need attention and guidance too. One day Angela said, "You have to let me go."

I told her, "You have to let me go too."

For a while we lost our connection; it was a difficult time. Now we are close, and she's the kind of mother and grandmother I wish I would have had growing up. Angela is also a talented actor, acting coach, and director. She gives me credit for who she has become, which I feel is the greatest compliment ever.

My youngest child, Dorian, got attention from his father that the others didn't get, and as a result, he was able to speak up for himself and had a lot more confidence. And that made it easy to not see what he was going through. It wasn't until much later that I learned how difficult it was for him to navigate the minefield that was our home. Being the youngest, Dorian saw what was happening with Angela and Joey and tried his best to be the "good kid." That meant walking on eggshells. When Dorian was born, Buddy gave him a lot of attention. He pushed Joey and Angela to the side, and for this Dorian paid a hefty price. Joey was hurt and picked on Dorian. I remember one incident stemming from the fact that Joey loved to play pool and wanted me to buy him a pool table, which I did. Chile, it sat right in the middle of our small living room. The kids loved it, and Joey could play with his friends when they came by. Well, Buddy decided to buy Dorian a pool stick but not Joey! He was so hurt that he took Dorian's pool stick and destroyed it. It wasn't Dorian's fault, but he paid for Buddy's insensitivity toward his big brother.

When I left Buddy, he tried using Dorian to get to me. Buddy would pretend he wanted to pick Dorian up to spend time with him, but he was really checking to see what I was doing. Once Dorian let him in, Buddy would go through my room to see what was in there. Dorian wasn't stupid. He soon picked up that his father was not coming for him. I'm sure it hurt him.

I blamed Dorian for telling his father where I lived and for letting him into the house. I wish I hadn't put that pressure on him. He was a kid, and it wasn't his fault. All my kids had to learn to keep secrets. That's what you put on them when they grow up in an unsafe home. The summer I left Detroit, only Angela knew we were leaving. She was fourteen, and she spent her last summer not being able to tell any of her friends goodbye. Joey didn't know; I couldn't risk Buddy finding out, so he was shocked when we left. By the age of thirteen, Dorian decided he did not want a relationship with his father and started to stay to himself. I guess it was also easier to pull away from me too; that way I couldn't blame him for shit he had nothing to do with.

When people found out there was a celebrity living in their neighborhood, Dorian felt responsible for protecting me. I mean, folks had no problem knocking on the door, wanting to meet me. Dorian was a buffer for me. But things got worse for him when some of his so-called friends broke into Angela's house. Dorian was so disappointed. It was a rude awakening that they were not his friends at all and, like his father, were only using him as a means to an end. In this case, robbing his family. Dorian cut them loose immediately, and now he was alone.

I fell for the first time in my life, and my attention turned to not only my boyfriend but his children as well. I even took one of his sons in and made Dorian share his room with him. So I helped make him feel even more invisible. He lost his voice and decided distancing himself was the only way to survive. Becoming a celebrity, with all the attention, events, and dinners, was overwhelming in the beginning. I wasn't balancing it well at first, and I know Dorian felt the neglect most of all.

The saying is "Love is blind." Well, honey, this describes me when I met the love of my life.

I've talked a lot about the abuse I experienced at the hands of my ex-husband and Angela's father. Fortunately that's not the end of my love story. I did get to experience being fully loved, and the memory of it has kept me going for years. I want to talk about this relationship so that you will know that love is possible, even if it is not perfect and even if it doesn't last. As the saying goes . . . "It's better to have loved and lost than never to have loved at all."

I met a man who was a concert pianist, actually through my daughter, Angela. It was during a festival in Watts that my daughter met him first and told him, "You have to meet my mother," and then she told me the same about him. She was playing Cupid, and it worked. There was this sparkle in his eyes the moment he saw me, and even though I did my best to remain cool and measured, I could feel something happening inside me that I had never felt before. I wasn't on television then; however, I was working as an actor in small independent films and working at United Airlines.

I fell in love with this man, and he reciprocated the love, and for the first time, I knew what it was like to be cherished. I also finally discovered why my friend Ruth used to rave about sex. I don't kiss and tell, but I will say that when you are a full-grown adult woman with adult children before you know what it's like to be sexually fulfilled, well, honey, you can lose your mind! By the time I learned this man was married, of course I was deeply in love, and my mind was blown. We laughed a lot, he courted me, I went to his concerts, and I have to tell you, I felt like a teenager. I hadn't felt this kind of protection or love or covering since my father. When this man finally told me about his wife, I felt betrayed and angry. I was lost and considered walking away many times, but my heart was not going to let me. I do believe that people come into your life for a reason, and he came to let me know that it was my season of knowing love was possible.

Horace Tapscott was my friend. His talent was undeniable, and he traveled the globe, playing the piano where his music was honored and lauded. He was most proud of the mentorship he created with the young, upcoming jazz musicians—both men and women—in his flagship organization, the Ark, also known as the Pan Afrikan Peoples Arkestra. Many renowned musicians came from his tutelage, and their regard for Horace was lifelong. Horace loved jazz, and his commitment to preserving the music was infectious. It inspired me to open a jazz club—that and wanting to have quality establishments in our community. Horace was present. He was romantic and supportive. He held my daughter's hand during her labor, my sons witnessed their mother become soft and feminine, and I saw what it meant to have a man look out for me. Horace had an aneurysm before I had mine. He walked several blocks from his home to my house one afternoon, and when I opened the door, he collapsed in my arms. The first hospital the paramedics took him to thought he was on drugs. They saw a Black man and figured he was OD'ing. I got him out of there and to Kaiser, where they saved his life. During this time, the doctor who performed the surgery told us the odds of Horace surviving were very low. The doctor's proclamation was very official in tone, and Horace's family seemed to accept that he wasn't going to make it.

His wife told me I didn't understand all the things he had been through. His sister handed me a Bible and guided me to read Mark 11:23: "For verily I say unto you, That whosoever shall say unto this mountain, Be thou removed, and be thou cast into the sea; and shall not doubt in his heart, but shall believe that those things which he saith shall come to pass; he shall have whatsoever he saith." I left them at the hospital and crossed the street to Founders Church of Religious Science. I sat downstairs and repeated this verse for two hours.

And then I said to God, "To show you that I believe what I'm saying, I'm not going back to the hospital. I'm going home." So that's what I did. I got in my bed, which for some reason felt very high that night, and went sound asleep.

When I woke up the next morning, I rushed back to the hospital, where the doctor said to me, "He's better, but we still have to do the surgery, because any little thing could trigger another aneurysm, and he will not survive." He went on to say, "The surgery is very dangerous and could leave him unable to walk or talk."

I told him, "I'm still going to pray that you don't have to do anything, and he can walk out of here." I said to God, "I asked you for his life, and that means he needs to walk, talk, and play the piano."

When Horace woke from the surgery, he told me, "I know you been here all night, so you better go home, and I'm going to call and make sure you do." I laughed and said to myself, *Well, he can talk*. And two weeks later he walked out of the hospital. Two months later he was doing a concert in New York!

During his time in the hospital, Horace believed he crossed over. He said it was such a peaceful experience that he almost stayed. He saw a lot of people he didn't recognize waiting for him, but he felt that he somehow knew them. He was given the option of coming back, so that's what he decided to do.

I told him, "Yeah, 'cause you know I was gonna have a fit!"

To that he replied, "I had the knowledge of you."

Horace was a man who loved women, and because of that he had five children, both inside and outside his marriage. I became close with most of the children through the years, and to this day they still call and check on me. His sister and his mother, affectionately called Mother Jackson, became part of my family as well. But the relationship that was the most enduring was with his wife, Cecilia.

Twenty years after his aneurysm, Horace was diagnosed with lung cancer, brought on because he was an avid smoker. And God forbid anyone try to tell him to stop smoking, doctor or not. I always felt he was afraid that he couldn't stop. Wanting to fix things as usual, I started researching every alternative option I could find. I knew world-renowned herbalist Dr. Sebi and believed that there were other healing modalities that could save Horace. I could tell that he wasn't hearing it. He was ready, because he believed he had already experienced crossing over, so he was unafraid. I stopped pushing and let it be. I was welcomed to visit his home when Horace was dying. After Horace made his transition, my first thought was to go be with Cecilia, but her son-in-law stopped me at the door and told me I should leave her alone and that I should be ashamed of myself. I was hurt but did what he asked. One day Cecilia called me, and she said, "I don't know what's taking me so long to call you and say I appreciate everything you did for me and Horace." I told her what her son-in-law said, and Cecilia replied, "We don't feel that way, and we told him that." Cecilia invited me to dinner, and after that we became very close. Her daughter Renee referred to me as "her girl." When I broke my foot, Cecilia came and sat with me. She would call to see what I was up to. We'd even go out together. We never let a week go by without speaking to each other. Over time her son-in-law saw our bond and one day came over and hugged me. Renee, his wife, told me he sent money for me to attend a concert that was in honor of Horace. I understood him, and I forgave him. Cecilia was a queen. She made her transition in April 2025. Horace is the only man I ever truly loved. Perhaps that is why our families blended so well. Or why Cecilia and I became close. Love was our bond.

Years after Horace died, I used my pendulum to speak with God, and I asked, "Did you send Horace to me?" And the answer was no. I was stunned, because it had felt so right all those years. So I apologized to my sons. I hadn't had enough self-worth back then to leave and wait on a love of my own. I had never thought it was even possible. Today I'd tell a woman to trust and wait on God to send her her own partner. To be intentional about what she wants in a partner. What does he bring? Does he respect you and keep his word? Is he loyal, a good listener, and a communicator?

Does he honor you? I'd tell her, *Don't be afraid to ask the hard questions up front.* Like, are you married? The way you start is how you will end. Back then I didn't know these things. I didn't ask questions; I was just happy to experience love on this level. After Horace, there was no one who could come close to making me feel as alive as I did with him. A few men came my way who were nice; however, I had already had the love of a lifetime, so I needed nothing after that.

Love is not just an emotion you hold for someone. Love is a verb! A verb that includes quality time, respect, patience, understanding, and communication. I learned this little by little. Sometimes it was painful. Hell, I think that as long as I am here, I'll be working on that.

CHAPTER SIX

Becoming Florence

Florence Johnston is the gift that keeps on giving. I loved portraying her. . . . She wasn't a prop. She had humanity and wit.

I'm most famous for a character who worked as a maid, who I played on a television show in the late 1970s and early '80s. The original part of Florence (the character's name) was a guest-starring role. But one thing led to another, and *boom*, a short-term gig became my launch into the realm of Hollywood stardom—and, most importantly, into a career as a working actor.

The show was called *The Jeffersons*, referring to the fictional couple who were its central characters. *The Jeffersons*, developed by Norman Lear, was a situation comedy about a married couple's pursuit of the American dream, an idea common to many of the stories told in film, television, and books. But it differed—and made history—from nearly every other thing television viewers saw at the time, because the main characters, the couple who rose up from being among the working poor, who moved on up to live the American dream, were Black. That was a new scenario for TV.

In the pilot, the first episode of season one, George and Louise Jefferson are relatively new to living in a high-rise apartment building in New York City's posh Upper East Side. They live with their only child, a son named Lionel. They have one Black neighbor, Helen Willis. She is married to a white man, with whom she lives, along with their only child, a daughter. Otherwise, the other Black people in and out of the building are workers, mostly maids and butlers. George Jefferson thinks that he and Louise should hire help, in keeping with their status. Louise is resistant to the idea. She is more comfortable doing her own housework, and—maybe more important—she knows what the work requires, because she worked as a maid when they were a younger couple working their way up. She isn't even comfortable telling a friend of hers, who continues to work as a maid, that she's a resident of the fancy high-rise. Louise invites her over and lets her assume at first that she's visiting Louise at a home where she is employed. In the meantime, George has gone to an agency to see about sending potential candidates for him and Louise to hire. They send me. Or, rather, they send Florence Johnston, played by me.

Louise's friend eventually finds out that she is interviewing maids and tells her she wants the job. When my character realizes this, she gladly relinquishes the job. Of course, Florence is on her best behavior in this pilot episode. As I'm heading out the door, looking at Roxie Roker's character, Helen, I ask, "Do you folks mind if I ask you something? You live in this building?" Helen says yes. Then, looking at Louise Jefferson, I ask, "You live in this building too?" Louise says yes. Totally baffled, I ask them both, "Well, how come we overcame, and nobody told me?"

The audience laughed for more than five minutes nonstop. The producers immediately wanted to know who I was. They were so amazed by the reaction that they decided right then and there to give me more to do. Next thing I knew, my agent told me that the show wanted me back. I still chuckle when I think about how Norman came to me later and said he couldn't get over the reaction of the audience, especially since "there were these two people who fell out into the aisle and could not stop laughing!" I knew they were my daughter and my boyfriend, but I decided to keep that to myself!

The producers wrote something else for me for the fifth episode—to see if they would get the same response. Then they wrote me into the eighth episode. Eventually I was offered a contract. Actress Pauline Myers had already been cast as Louise and George's maid. She was confident she was going to be a regular on the show. I was just happy to be there. But then, when they started calling me back and eventually gave the role to me, I heard that Pauline said she "didn't want to do that kind of stuff anyway." She was referring to the way the character Florence spoke.

Pauline didn't want to speak with what she felt was "ghetto" English; she wanted to speak properly, like Roxie and Isabel. I got that, but my perspective was different. I was fine with the way Florence spoke. I didn't see it as an unintelligent way of speaking, nor inconsistent with reality. In developing the character for myself, I was pulling from my experience with my grandmother and aunt, who had been maids. I emulated them. Ironically, when I got *The Jeffersons* and one of the producers, Bernie West, showed me the photo that made them call me in, it was the one with the broom that Lil Cumber had made me take. I had pushed back against her idea for me to look like a maid, just like Pauline had. I guess Lil did know what she was talking about.

I went on to do more successful and even groundbreaking television shows, films, and other kinds of projects in business, art, and culture. But my time on *The Jeffersons*—one decade of my life—marked a turning point for me professionally and personally, as I also lived the life of a working mother and an engaged member of my community. Like in the classic theme song of the show, the decade

I performed in the role of Florence Johnston marked the season when I moved on up from some pretty low and challenging stuff in my work and in my personal life.

Norman Lear, a white American writer and producer, was known for successful shows that shook things up, brought new ideas and voices to popular storytelling, and made television that was also top-rated. He was a Kennedy Center Honoree (2017), a recipient of the National Medal of Arts (1999), and so much more. He had a production company called ACT III and was behind shows that earned him numerous Emmy Awards. He is best known for iconic television shows of the 1970s and 1980s, including *All in the Family*, *Maude*, *Good Times*, and of course *The Jeffersons*. To quote former president Bill Clinton (in 1999), "Norman Lear has held up a mirror to American society and changed the way we look at it." Lear saw the value of including all of the stories that make our country unique. *The Jeffersons* is an important part of his legacy. It is also, I'm proud to say, a part of my legacy and my story as a working actor as well. That said, getting hired by him was not easy for me. I was a hardworking artist with a day job that allowed me to support my family and household of three children on one income.

George and Louise had been neighbors of Archie Bunker, the central character in *All in the Family*, in Queens, where they'd lived before moving on up. They'd started out in Harlem, where Louise sometimes did daywork and George held down a low-level job at a dry cleaner. He learned the business from the inside out and ultimately opened not one but seven dry cleaners, including, he would say, "One near you!" He was the quintessential entrepreneur who pulled himself up by his bootstraps. He was brash and opinionated—the mirror image of Archie in politics and social perspective. He was meant to be a racist—the Black version. Louise was a loving wife, bringing a balance and the beauty of femininity to the couple; she was not the shrinking violet that Edith, Archie Bunker's wife, was. She had opinions, which she expressed, and busted George's chops when necessary. The Jeffersons, as a couple, displayed Black swagger and style. George's was particularly exaggerated. No one could do the George Jefferson walk nor deliver lines that bent people over in laughter the way Sherman Hemsley did.

Sherman Hemsley was good at setting me up for a comeback. In one particular episode, he said, "I'm an executive"—as opposed to a low-level worker such as his maid. "Well here, take out the garbage."

I, as Florence, picked up the garbage pail and said, "Well, hop in."

Florence recognized the accomplishments of her employers relative to her own and treated them with respect and as equals, especially in the sense that she didn't hide her humanity. She brought her whole self to work. She was an intelligent, normal, and unattached woman in New York City in the 1970s and '80s.

One of my favorite episodes is "Florence in Love." Robert DoQui, a prominent actor, played my boyfriend. The story goes, there's a rainstorm in New York that is so bad, he can't take the bus home. Florence allows him to spend the night. She puts him in her bedroom, and she sleeps on the couch so that in the morning, when the Jeffersons awake, she will be there to explain what happened. The producers wanted the man to be in the bedroom with me, but I didn't feel Florence would do that. The director took me to the exec producers and said, "Marla has a problem. Mind you, I don't know if we want to solve it." He was setting me up to get a no.

It so happened my favorite exec producer, Don Nicholl, asked, "What is the problem, Marla?" I had learned that any time you're asked a question by an authority figure, you turn it around and ask them a question.

So I asked, "Why is it important to you to have the man in Florence's bedroom?"

Don answered, "We thought it would be fun."

I said "What's fun about it? I'm disrespecting their home, they have a son in the house, and Florence can't think of anything better to do than have a man in her bedroom?" I then went on to explain how Florence (as most Black girls in that day) grew up. "You were never allowed to have company in your bedroom, and if they were in there, no one—I mean, no one—ever sat on your bed." I looked Don in the eyes and asked, "Would you want a strange man in your house even sleeping on your sofa?"

Don said, "No, no I wouldn't. We'll change the line." And they did.

What happens is, the Jeffersons wake up, and when Louise goes into the kitchen to get some coffee, she sees a man in George's robe sitting behind a newspaper. Louise thinks it's George until she pulls his newspaper down to make him answer her. Louise screams, and all hell breaks loose. George is upset and calls me immoral because he thinks I slept with the man. George fires Florence, who promptly lets him know that "for your information, T. J. slept in the bedroom, and I slept on the couch, so you can't fire me, 'cause I quit." This episode was so much fun to do because I got a chance to do some over-the-top physical comedy. Mr. Willis tries to get George to hire me back by lying, telling him Florence had to go back to Mississippi and live a hard life. George agrees to bring me back if I will behave like a proper maid, including no talking back. So Florence comes back and shows him what a proper maid looks and acts like. I borrow from the character of Prissy, played by Butterfly McQueen, in *Gone with the Wind*. I wear the stereotypical maid outfit, headscarf and all. I follow George around and will not let him rest. His every wish is my command. I call him "Massa," make his drinks, sing "Old Folks at Home," and attempt to shine his shoes.

George gets upset and says, "Get off me!"

To which I cry, "Oh lordy me, I done made you mad." Then I grab his knees and beg for forgiveness, during which the doorbell rings, so I stay on my knees and wobble to the door, saying, "I'll get it, I'll get it." By the end George is so exhausted with me that he begs me to stop. I immediately revert back to my old self with "Say please." Sherman and I had a ball bouncing off each other. We had such great chemistry together. Sherman Hemsley was one of the most generous costars I ever worked with.

My character was meant to keep him in check—keep him humble, so to speak. You can draw laughter without being demeaning and while making a point. Any time you place a stigma on someone because they are of a certain race, religion, gender, or income, you're doing it to yourself. When you point at me, there are four fingers pointing back at you. He happily set me up so that I could slam him, and I did the same for him. We worked together so well. He was hilarious. Our rhythms were compatible. Sometimes he would say to me, "You know, Marla, I forgot my lines. I don't know my lines!"

I'd tell him, "Yes, you do. Your mind took a picture of them the first time we did it. So stop saying you don't know them." In other words, I was encouraging him to be confident in what he knew. Maybe he hadn't studied his lines as much as he usually did. But his mind had registered what he'd read already. So don't doubt yourself. Thoughts become things. So think of yourself as successfully doing a thing, not failing.

On *The Jeffersons*, I had the pleasure of working with actors whose work I was a fan of, like Billy Dee Williams, Lee Weaver, Thalmus Rasulala, Beah Richards, Peter Lawford, and my first teacher, Lillian Randolph.

Another favorite episode had Billy Dee Williams as a guest. Florence meets the doorman, played by Ned Wertimer, who gives her a card from a celebrity doubles agency for George, who was going to use a double as a backup in case he couldn't land Billy Dee. But as it turns out, he was able to get the real one to come, but Florence doesn't know it. When Billy Dee arrives, Florence—unlike Louise and Helen, who are dressed to the nines in his favorite color, blue—comes out in a bathrobe, rollers, and a headscarf. Florence is somewhat of an aficionado of all things Billy Dee. She proceeds to drill him. "What's your favorite food?" "In *Lady Sings the Blues*, did Diana Ross wear the flower on the left side or the right?" Of course, he gets none of the answers right. Meanwhile, Helen and Louise are taking pictures with and swooning all over Billy. Finally the doorman comes to deliver Billy's wallet, which he accidentally left in the cab. Florence grabs it and says, "Let me see who you really are, Mister . . . Mister . . ." Her mouth opens in shock when she realizes it's really him.

Billy holds his hand out for the wallet and says, "Do you want my arm to fall off?"

Florence loses it. "What did you say? That's the same thing he said to Diana Ross in *Lady Sings the Blues*!" Then she runs to the balcony and shouts, "BILLY DEE IS UP HERE, Y'ALL!!" Next she begs him to stay while she puts on her blue dress, but he can't, so she grabs him and begs, "Don't leave me now!!!" It was hysterical, and Billy and I had a ball and did our best to keep from making each other laugh.

I didn't know that the director had cooked up a kiss between Billy and me. So, at the end, Billy walks up to me, holds my face in his hands, leans in, and kisses me. Both Florence and Marla were in shock! Billy says, "Ciao bella." As soon as he leaves, Florence screams and faints. The fans loved this episode so much, it became a classic.

Working on *The Jeffersons* was a dream come true. I would often play with Sherman and Isabel between takes. Sherman had a habit of hiding food on the counter in the kitchen when that set wasn't being used. I would move his snacks, so that when he reached in to grab them, they wouldn't be there. Isabel would put her stuff in cabinets, and I would wait until she wasn't looking and move them. I loved to mess with them. The entire cast was like a family.

The Jeffersons's first episode was broadcast in 1975, and from there it had a ten-year run. Thanks to advancements in technology and the way audiences view television and film, the show has been available to viewers since the eighties. New generations of people have discovered the show and continue to watch, to laugh, and to tell me and those who worked on the show with me how much our work means to them.

I'm not a comedian. I'm actually quite a serious person. But the more serious you are about a thing, the funnier the situations you find yourself in. Imagination can't beat real life when it comes to delivering the funny. If you really deal with truth, you get humor.

"Black people speak in a rhythm. Chinese people speak in a rhythm. Jewish people punch words a lot." I would say on set that I had to say the lines in my rhythm. After a while I was able to turn the one laugh I got from the audience per show into two or three. So I was left alone to do what I do.

The show was fictional and meant to entertain. I was playing a maid, one of the most common stereotypes of Black women in TV and film. But my character was not behaving in the stereotypical ways that characters played by actors before me, such as Hattie McDaniel and Butterfly McQueen, who both appeared in *Gone with the Wind*, had. Nor was my character like Beulah, the name of a character on the same-titled show that came before us. Florence was not self-deprecating nor deferential. She showed respect to her employers, including calling them Mr. and Mrs. Jefferson. She attended to her work. But she had opinions and freely expressed them. She got in her bosses' business, not in a "Are we sick, boss?" way (as it was in *Gone with the Wind*), but rather to save them from themselves and have their backs—even when her good intentions led to things going wrong.

There are subtleties in making television that make a

production sing. Costuming, makeup, the surroundings of the characters, the stage set, and the design. The episode where I borrowed Butterfly McQueen's costume was even more effective because the dress was so different from what Florence wore and how she usually presented herself. The costume spoke so loudly, I didn't have to say much to get the point across. Otherwise, Florence wore dresses that were fitting for a working woman in the mid-sixties to mid-seventies: shirtdresses and slim shifts. Her hair was natural through some seasons, and in others I wore wigs with straight, short, neat cuts. Isabel and Roxie's characters, being ladies who lunch and all, were more glamorous. They were both beautiful dark-brown women with very different body types. Helen's daughter was a bit lighter and brought the energy and fashion that was trendier and more in line with what younger people were wearing. Lionel did too. The men, of course, wore their uniforms, from the doorman in his cap to George in his three-piece suit that went along with his big-man swagger.

Adella Farmar, a Black woman, was in charge of our costumes. Most of what we wore was custom-made. Not so much working with designer names like today. That cost more than the producers wanted to spend. Nonetheless, we looked great all the time. Adella and I became great friends. Our children knew each other. She had previously worked on *Good Times* and would go on to work on *ER*. Ray Hall, a Black man, kept our hair looking camera-worthy. Even when he had to use paint and somebody else's hair to do it. In fact, Isabel, Roxie, and I all agreed that during our time with Ray, our hair was healthy and grew longer than we had ever experienced.

The ensemble of actors on *The Jeffersons* brought a tremendous collective body of work and experience. Isabel Sanford had a more-than-thirty-year career in the theater. She had appeared in the film *Guess Who's Coming to Dinner*, starring Sidney Poitier and Katharine Hepburn.

Isabel as Louise, aka Weezy, once a working wife, represented the women of the world, Black or otherwise, who could afford to donate their time to philanthropic efforts. Lionel, their son—most memorably played by Mike Evans, though two others portrayed him—represented an intelligent and caring Black youth. And Zara Cully, aka Mother Jefferson, represented our elders as a most buttoned-up, proper Black lady, born to torment her daughter-in-law.

Some of us were more closely living the lives of the people we were playing than others. When Norman hired Roxie Roker, he said, "Now, for this part, you're married to a white man, and you're going to be required to kiss him. Is that all right?" he asked her.

Roxie said, "Let me put it to you this way." She reached into her bag and pulled out a photo of her real, also white, husband to show him. Our show made history for being one of the first on primetime television to show an interracial kiss when Franklin Cover and Roxie did so, and there was, of course, pushback. The two of them became good friends and were a lot of fun to work with, together and separately. Roxie was Franklin's regular ride to work. Consequently she called him "the Black woman's burden."

Franklin was married to a white woman in real life. He'd been a stage actor too, doing classical work, including Shakespeare. He would go on to have a forty-year career and star in *Wall Street*, *The Stepford Wives*, and *Almost Heroes*. He passed away in 2006.

I loved Roxie. We took tennis lessons together with this guy from Inglewood, and all we did was run for the ball. She joined a spa and took me there. When she wanted to try something new, she wanted me to do it with her. I got to know her family, including her talented son, Lenny Kravitz, who would visit on set.

Roxie had previously appeared in *ABC Afterschool Specials* on television, but like Sherman, she had a deep experience with the Negro Ensemble Company (NEC). The organization of Black actors produced plays and were actively engaged in getting themselves and a talented group of Black actors jobs in the industry. It was founded in 1965 by a circle of artists, including playwright Douglas Turner Ward, producer/actor Robert Hooks, and theater manager Gerald Krone.

Paul Benedict was our castmate in the role of the Jeffersons' eccentric English next-door neighbor. Paul had tons of experience in comedy before working with us, including many projects with Norman, from the early 1970s up through guest appearances on *All in the Family* and *Maude*. Ned Wertimer played the doorman. While that became his most famous role, he also appeared in *Bad Company* right after *The Jeffersons*, and *Pirates of the Caribbean: At World's End* and more years later.

Sherman had worked in a post office in New York to sustain himself early on in his acting career. He moved to LA when Norman offered him a role on *All in the Family*.

Mother Jefferson was played by Zara Cully, who'd had appeared on that show as well. She had worked in local theater in Jacksonville, Florida, where she had lived, as an educator, actor, director, and more. She and I alternated because she was the nemesis to Louise, and I was the nemesis to George. I just loved Zara. She had such a rich history in the business. In fact, she was dubbed Dame Zara Cully by the theater community. One day she brought in pictures from all the shows she had performed in; it was amazing.

Berlinda Tolbert, a former Broadway performer, played Jenny Willis, the daughter of our neighbors, who marries the Jeffersons' son, Lionel. Lionel was played predominantly by two actors, both named Evans but not related. There was Mike Evans and Damon Evans. Damon made his Broadway debut in *The Me Nobody Knows*. He was also in *Via Galactica* and toured as Judas and Jesus Christ in the concert version of the musical *Jesus Christ Superstar*.

Mike Evans was Lionel before Damon. He had worked in the business and with Norman Lear as an actor and writer. He played a friend of Archie Bunker's daughter, Gloria, in *All in the Family*. He wrote for the other Black sitcom by Lear, *Good Times*.

I continued to do theater while working in television when I could, because I loved it. But every actor knows that unless you're doing Broadway or regional theater, earning enough in theater to make a good living is very difficult. I was lucky where money and this career opportunity were concerned because filming *The Jeffersons* was close to doing theater. We shot live with an audience. So I felt at home.

People who came from theater to TV always did well because they were used to having to be spontaneous in front of a live audience and accustomed to blocking, or knowing the predesignated places and positions where they needed to be in to connect with an audience. You needed to appear to move through a scene naturally but not turn your back on the camera and the audience—even when giving another character a hug.

When the director looked to block me in a scene, I would already be where he was going to place me. He'd see me in place and say, "Marla. Oh, yeah, that's good right there." I wasn't just there to do my part. I paid attention to what the sound supervisor and assistants were doing, what grips did, how the set designers were creating the world. I watched everybody. I was there to understand how a show was produced, top to bottom. Little did I know how handy this would come in later.

Before actors get to a set on a soundstage to rehearse and perform, they read their scripts aloud together around a table. So it's appropriately called a table read. In addition to the actors, producers, directors, and other executives may attend as well. Once the script is read by the actors, they often leave the room so that the writers and others who remain can suggest changes and tweaks as they might see fit. I was naturally inclined to stay at the table to hear what the execs discussed. Against custom, they didn't ask me to leave. *The Jeffersons* was a new show. Maybe they didn't want to be rude.

I did find myself having something to say. I interjected, "Excuse me, Black people don't talk like that." The writers were mostly men and Jewish, and that made a difference in how they heard and spoke language. They would, for example, punch a joke in the manner that people spoke in their cultures and communities. Black people don't punch in the way they deliver the funny; they throw away what they say. We also have a unique rhythm and style to the way we speak. Like, "Child, if you don't sit your butt down, I'll knock you into tomorrow."

Not everyone responded positively to me staying at the table and speaking up, though. Other cast members warned me to essentially stay in my place, saying, "If there's something wrong [with the script], the producers will see it." I was breaking protocol, but I was speaking out, with good reason.

I'd say to them, "Yeah, but I've never heard anybody say, 'It's bad writing,' when a performance isn't going down well with an audience. They usually say, 'She can't act.'" I was looking out for my self-interest as an actor. I was not about to let anyone say that about me. I sat at the table to make sure they got my part right.

Before long our producers let all of the actors sit at the table. A new tradition started with our show. It only made sense that writers know what an actor's thoughts are about the words they're obliged to read. Don Nicholl, one of our head writers, often asked my opinion of a joke and for another word to use to make something funny. He trusted my judgment.

I considered how our viewers and fans would respond to what we said, how we said it, and how we presented our characters. And as I got more comfortable in my role on the show, I wanted writers to be careful about the things they wrote for my character. If what they wrote resembled nothing I thought someone would actually say in real life, I told them so. I wanted realism and authenticity. Florence was meant to be sassy in the way she talked to Mr. Jefferson, but I didn't want her to dump on him all the time. It would come off as disrespectful.

One of my most remarked-about strengths was my timing. They said I had great timing. But at the time, I didn't know what they meant. Now I know that the successful delivery of a line depends on a certain rhythm and vocal inflection. Spoken sentences don't end up. They end down. When I would hear one of my castmates end their line with an up tone as if they were asking a question, they wouldn't get a laugh. It made a difference. When you end your sentence up, the audience is waiting to hear what else you have to say, and they don't laugh.

Monday was dress rehearsal day, when we worked in our wardrobe and did a run-through. Tuesday was the day we'd film the same episode for two different audiences. All the other days were rehearsals. At United—where, yes, I was still working—I had seniority, so when we picked our shifts, I would always pick Monday and Tuesday or Saturday and Sunday. Most of the employees wanted the weekends off, so this way it was easy for me to trade for the days I wanted.

The Jeffersons brought me money and notoriety, but I wasn't so famous that my family and I couldn't continue living a normal life. People in general didn't recognize me when I was out and about or at my day job, not after only seven episodes in the first season. There would be times when a customer would call in and say they recognized my voice, but they just couldn't place it. I worked part-time and in the evenings. We got off the set at five or six o'clock. We taped at the KTTV studios located on Wilton and Sunset. The 101 freeway was one block over, so I would take it to the Wilshire Boulevard and Sixth Street exit, where United Airlines was located in Los Angeles. This made it very easy to live the double life working both TV and my day job.

At the time the company was having a problem with one of my coworkers. She worked the midnight shift and was often coming in late. The manager then asked me to stay an hour later. I suggested that I move my schedule up by coming in an hour later and leaving regularly at midnight. If the often-late employee fell behind, I would already be there. They agreed. This also worked out for me during those times when *The Jeffersons* rehearsals ran over.

My life was starting to make sense and feel good for the first time. I was trusting in God completely and feeling loved. I had my children in a new house. I was happy we were all together again. But even with the popularity of the show, I still didn't feel like I'd made it. Because today you're working, and tomorrow you ain't, child. That's just the way life is, especially in the entertainment business. I've seen people with great acting skills who were once on television and who are now no longer working. You can't be in a fantasy about this business.

By the sixth season, I moved up from number nine in the ranks of *The Jeffersons* to number three, right behind Isabel Sanford and Sherman Hemsley. I learned, though, that I wasn't making half of what the leads were getting, and yet I was carrying the same load.

I asked Roxie how much she was paid. As Helen Willis, she was a member of the supporting cast but an important player in the ensemble. She avoided directly answering and suggested, rather, that I talk to my agent about money. I raised the subject with her because I thought the time had come for the support cast, including me, to receive a salary increase.

I shared with her what I was making, and she was floored by it. And I'm certain that our show executives thought they were doing well by me. They had seen what I was making at United Airlines.

Roxie then suggested that she and I talk with Franklin Cover. The three of us talked, and in our conversation, I agreed to write a letter on behalf of the entire supporting cast to request a meeting about what we were being paid. We didn't leave the leading cast out. But when I went to Isabel, she said, "I don't believe in making waves." We knew already that Sherman wouldn't join us in speaking out on the matter. But then they were the exceptions among us actors. They were making the top salaries. My agent told me that the producers called to say, "Marla is not going to make trouble, is she?"

I responded to my agent, "Yes. Yes, she is." My agent was concerned that I might put my job at risk, but she stood in support of us anyway. If the executives had let me go for challenging their pay practices, the show would suffer consequences where they least wanted it to. The legions of people who were fans of the show loved Florence. And the audience would not be pleased. Plus, we were not asking to be given anything; we had already earned the right for more. They did not agree to a meeting, but rather, they did offer us an increase in residual payouts.

I shared this with the other cast members and said, "This is not what we asked for. We asked for a meeting." We stood our ground and got the meeting. By now Paul Benedict, aka Mr. Bentley; Ned Wertimer, aka Ralph the doorman; and Berlinda Tolbert had joined the efforts of the cast.

One of the first things said to us at the meeting was "Marla, we already gave you a little something."

"That's the key phrase," I said. "'A little something.' But you're not giving me what Isabel and Sherman are getting, and you're asking me to do everything they do and more. You ought to at least give me fifty percent of what they get."

Ultimately I got what I asked for out of the meeting. We all received more. Berlinda, who had all but been written out of the show, also got more episodes.

Two years into my working on *The Jeffersons*, one of the producers, Bernie West, asked, "Do you still have that job?"

"Yeah."

"We thought you'd quit. Aren't you tired?"

"You ain't told me nothing to make me quit. You got something to tell me?"

"Would you be willing to take a leave of absence?" he asked.

"I'll take a leave if you pay me."

As I thought about the number I would ask for, I felt embarrassed at the thought of them knowing how little I actually made at my day job. I gave them the number I wanted, though. And they said yes. They'd pay it, and I would take a ninety-day leave from United. I took the ninety days plus. I never returned to work at the airline again. Before I left, I proposed that I be a spokesperson for them, but they declined. So that was that: No more "This is United Airlines . . . May I help you?" No more day job, side job, freelance job. I was now a full-time paid actor.

CHAPTER SEVEN

Lights, Camera, Breakthrough

Unbeknownst to me, though,
I was walking an uncharted path.
I was breaking barriers and making
history in the industry for women
and for people of color.

My family was on stable ground; my children grew up and found their own paths forward.

My life took me from being a Midwestern working wife and mom who baked cookies and hosted parties for the children in my Detroit home to being a single mother of three behind the scenes in Los Angeles when I wasn't working on a soundstage or being broadcast to the world on primetime television.

Not long before I landed the role on *The Jeffersons*, Angela graduated from Los Angeles High School (after initially going to Fairfax High), and against my judgment, she went across the country to Washington, DC, for college at Howard University. She was really striking out on her own and experiencing life as a young adult. I, though, was not ready. I'd been holding her close all this time. I was trying not to let my baby girl go far from me.

Angela had always been a leader; even among her peers as children, she'd take the initiative to make things happen. She had her own mind and was good at being a caretaker of others—and at an early age. She was strong before it should have been time to be.

Maybe all of that caretaking of others, including of me, was why she needed to be away from us for a while. Sometimes I might have leaned on her too much. I always wanted happiness for her and good people in her life. I clung to her and felt jealous of her friendships. Her brothers missed her too. Mother-daughter relationships can be a trip, honey.

She did great at Howard and met her spiritual conscious tribe. She also met a man whom she fell in love with, and she gave me my first grandchild—a son named Amil. Unfortunately Amil's father began showing signs of what would later be a schizophrenia diagnosis, so Angela left Howard and Washington, DC, behind to return home with Amil. I was happy they both were at home and close to our family. A lot of times people give me credit for the work my daughter's done. But Angela was the one behind many of the great decisions I made in the arts and in business.

Joey was spreading his wings, but closer to home. Abuse by people and drug use took him to hell and back. He was returning to himself and moved into the back house on my property. Brilliant and full of energy like his sister and younger brother, he received a broker's license and has been running a real estate business for many years.

We four went through a lot together that could have broken our trust and relationships, but we got through it. Sometimes I didn't know what might come of us as a family. But we were blessed. We continue to be blessed. And we all continue to praise God. An attitude of gratitude goes a long way.

The Jeffersons was in its seventh season when network executives proposed another spin-off, this one called *Checking In*. My character, Florence Johnston, in the new storyline, moves on up from working for a private household to working with a big staff serving the public. The show's title, *Checking In*, refers to a fictional St. Frederick Hotel in New York City. Florence is an executive housekeeper. A promotion of sorts. A career leap too. I was now moving from playing a supporting role to being the lead. This was my show.

That was great. But it wasn't everything required for me to say yes to the opportunity. I would only agree to accept the role if two conditions were met: I needed to be allowed to return to *The Jeffersons* and have at least the salary I had before, should *Checking In* fail in the ratings. And I needed to be allowed to research the character and make input on her development for the script. It was important to me to well represent real people in the world who do the work and live regular lives. I'd already picked up on aspects of what the creators of the show came up with that didn't quite sit right with me.

They initially saw this new Florence as a high-profile woman. I pushed back, saying that "I need to meet an executive housekeeper in real life and see what she does." The executives were in agreement and sent me to the Ambassador Hotel and the Century Plaza, both in Los Angeles. I shadowed the head of housekeeping around.

Once I had more information and time to consider how I would play the character, production on the show began, directed by Jack Shea. He had worked on *The Jeffersons* and later worked on *Designing Women* when it launched in 1986.

The team of actors I worked with included Larry Linville, known as the doctor Major Frank Burns on *M*A*S*H*; the Emmy-winning Liz Torres, a comedic actress; singer Ruth Brown; and Robert Costanzo, who played a role on *Hill Street Blues*, which also broadcast in 1981. The ensemble was great and made me proud. My son Joey was also cast in a role playing the character Dennis.

The show aired only four episodes, from April 9 through April 30, 1981. I had concerns about the show's two executive producers. They had come out of Norman Lear's camp. I asked Norman to reconsider bringing them on board, but he gave them to me anyway. While we were shooting, those guys were out on the beach, flirting with girls instead of writing.

I'm sure Norman initially thought he'd made a good decision. But at some point, he changed his mind. Norman came to me not too long after and said, "I wouldn't care if you decided not to do the show. It's up to you."

Despite my reservations, I went through with it. I didn't want to disappoint my cast members—whom I had tremendous respect for—nor deprive them of expected income. Adding insult to injury on the show, the Writers Guild of America (WGA) then voted to strike. Cable television and home video had opened up new markets and ways of making greater profit for the television industry. Not unlike what's happened in recent times with the advent of streaming, big business found new forms of income. The newfound profit wasn't trickling down to the writers. So they stopped working and started picketing. The strike lasted for three months. Up to that time, our execs had written the four shows but nothing more.

The final episode of the seventh season of *The Jeffersons* was titled "Florence's New Job," teasing the new show.

The Jeffersons writers had to scramble to write me back

into the show. I was so grateful that I'd had a contractual stipulation allowing me to return. And mostly grateful to friends in the business who shared their experiences with me, so I was educated on how to negotiate. Whitman Mayo, who appeared on *Sanford and Son* as the character Grady Wilson—sidekick of the main character, Fred Sanford—was offered a spin-off three years into the show. The show *Grady* lasted for ten episodes but was not brought back. Whitman did get the chance to return to *Sanford and Son*, but not at the same salary he had left with. He had to come back as if he was new to the show. It was a financial setback and felt like he was starting over. He shared that painful experience with me, and I remembered it and made sure that my agent negotiated a contract for *Checking In* that would insist that my prior salary be restored if I returned to *The Jeffersons*. God bless the child who pays attention and stands up for the right to decent compensation. They will be blessed with more to share.

The Jeffersons changed time slots at least fifteen different times during its eleven-season run. This was not a common practice for a popular, long-running series. It became hard for people to find us, and ratings dipped when the times switched up. In the first season (1974–75), the show ranked at number three, close behind *All in the Family*, which it was spun off from. The subsequent years our show would rise and fall but always stay in the top thirty. I'm proud to say I was part of a show that received fourteen Emmy Award nominations. I was nominated for Outstanding Supporting Actress in a Comedy Series from 1981 to 1985, each year, but I never won.

Checking In, the offspring, had a short life. The run of *The Jeffersons* ended in 1985, after a decade on air. Me, I kept on keeping on.

I would soon have another opportunity of a lifetime. A television show that was closer to home, so to speak—a stage play called *Two Twenty Seven*, written by playwright Christine Houston, who had won a Norman Lear writing contest and had written episodes of *The Jeffersons*. There were no years in between *The Jeffersons* and *227*. The door of *The Jeffersons* closed, but in no time, new doors opened.

My daughter, Angela, and I had shared visions of creating spaces and opportunities to support the cultural and economic health of our communities and artists and took the steps to manifest our ambitions. (I'll share more on that larger vision in a bit.)

Angela launched a theater company called Crossroads in 1981, where we put on a production of the play *Two Twenty Seven*, and it was sold and turned into a series called *227*, right behind *The Jeffersons*. My son Jordan was working in sound at the studio lot, and my other son, Dorian, was developing a unique apartment building idea he came up with. He also wrote an episode of *227*.

The *Two Twenty Seven* play originally premiered at San

Jose State University in 1983. Angela was introduced to it by renowned director Edmund Cambridge. Edmund, a founding member of the Negro Ensemble Company, taught at the Kilpatrick-Cambridge Theater Arts. Angela read the play and was not only impressed by it; she thought that it was perfect for me to play the lead. The story was about a woman named Mary, a working-class Black woman living in a small apartment building in Chicago, among her family and neighbors. Angela and Shay Wafer, her college roommate from Howard University, produced the play.

Shay, a graduate of a Yale University master's program, went on to helm several theaters, including the St. Louis Black Rep and the August Wilson Theatre. Now she is the executive director of Tina Knowles's theater, WACO. I wish I could say that I welcomed Shay joining our team. Shay and Angela were great friends, and I found myself intimidated by their closeness. I acted the role of a possessive mother sometimes. I was not happy, for example, when Angela chose to go across the country to attend Howard University. I wanted her to go to school in California. I loved her and had also become dependent on her in ways that might have felt confining. We parents are required to let our children go their own way in life. It's frightening for most people and causes us to act out of character. I was jealous, and sometimes, let's just say, I could be less than loving to my daughter's good friend, a person who dedicated herself to a common goal with us.

Shay believed in *227* enough to quit her job and join Angela to open the doors to Crossroads in 1982. The story portrayed the lives of Black lower-class tenants in 1950s Chicago—the hardships they faced back then. Chicago was also my birthplace, and I very closely related to the story. I took Angela's advice and joined the cast. Our director, Edmund, brought Hal Williams and Rosie Lee Hooks to the production.

A role opened up in the cast when one of the leads, Audrey Cobb, an amazing talent, left the play. I thought my stepsister, Susie Garrett, would be great to replace her in the role. So I flew Susie out to California from Detroit.

My sister from another father, Susie wasn't a trained actress. But I knew that she was hysterical, and I was confident that she could perform well and be great in this play. Susie and I would sit on the stoop of the apartment and gossip and play the numbers in real life. The play was reflecting that reality.

Susie wasn't as certain as I was that she could be a performer onstage, but I convinced her. She had a hard time believing she could do it, but I wasn't going to let her back out.

Just as I thought, we had a chemistry on set that was perfectly in sync. We could read each other's minds. I knew when she was about to go off script, and I was ready for her, but she was ready for me too. Susie got so good that one of the executives from Norman's staff said to me, "Marla, she's stealing the show." I told her, "That's okay, 'cause I got a contract." I was thrilled. And it got better. The play *Two Twenty Seven* was a theatrical hit; everybody was hearing about it.

Initially we thought *Two Twenty Seven* would run for a couple of months. But its popularity grew, and people kept coming. We'd been prepared to do a short run and move on to other projects. We had already made a deal for another play to follow *Two Twenty Seven*. We had to take it down, though, and extend the run of *Two Twenty Seven*. In the sixth month of the actual run, we caught the attention of many industry insiders, like Fuller Gordy, Roy Campanella II, and writer, producer, and actor Scoey Mitchell.

Scoey brought Brandon Tartikoff, the president of NBC Entertainment, to the play. I didn't know who Tartikoff he was. I found out, though, that night after the show. "I want you to meet Brandon," Scoey said, at the man's side.

I, not knowing any better, simply greeted him and said, "Thank you for coming," before I soon left. I'm sure Scoey and Brandon were wondering what was wrong with me that I hadn't seized the moment of opportunity. Nonetheless, when Tartikoff saw Susie's performance, he offered her a role on the TV series *Punky Brewster*. Susie played Betty, who was Cherie Johnson's grandma and also the surrogate mom to Punky.

Norman Lear ran into me on the lot and said, "I hear you have a hit show. I want to see it."

"Well, you better come tomorrow, because we're closing."

Norman showed up with his wife and some of his production staff. The house was packed by the time they arrived, so they had to sit way in the back. He was impressed. Afterward Norman wanted to know what we were doing with the play and if I had signed anything. I told him that we'd had a meeting with Columbia but hadn't signed agreements. There had been no talk of money yet.

He asked me to schedule a meeting with him. I did, and that's when he suggested that he and I team up on the project. Norman saw it as a Broadway play. I saw it as a movie of the week. Either way, he'd underwrite the expenses for us to remount the show and invite CBS to consider broadcasting it. CBS passed on the project, though. With that, I reminded Norman that NBC Entertainment's president, Brandon Tartikoff, had seen our production of *Two Twenty Seven* as well, and he saw it as a series.

While we were working to get the television rights to the play *Two Twenty Seven*, producer Roy Campanella II was also attempting to do the same. In fact, Christine told me she'd already promised the rights to him. Christine decided to have us all share the rights, because she wanted to have them as well. Roy said he had a deal brewing at Columbia Pictures for the project. We had a meeting with him and the guy who was going to be the executive producer. I told them I wanted Christine to be involved because she'd created the play.

The exec producer responded with "Well, I work alone."

When the meeting was over and I got outside, I told Roy, "Well, he will be working alone, but he won't be working on *Two Twenty Seven*."

We needed to make the play relevant to a new audience through a new medium: a soundstage, a live audience, watching us record a show for broadcast to everyone with access to a television.

The apartment building that was our set and fictional home had a large front stoop that was the center of most of the talk that drove the action in an episode. The interior rooms looked like they were from the 1980s, as did our wardrobe, hair, and makeup. The themes of the episodes needed to speak to the current times. Hardworking people were still faced with challenges to make ends meet and to get along, but we were now in the post–Civil Rights phase of things. The HIV/AIDS epidemic was destroying lives everywhere, especially in the arts, in addition to the drug trade tearing apart households and communities. There was a lot to talk about in the world through the arts, including through television.

Norman was building an empire in television. Besides *The Jeffersons*, *Checking In*, and more, it included a TV show that put Archie Bunker's wife's cousin Maude Findlay at its center. The star was Bea Arthur, and the show was called *Maude*. She was very different from the quiet, deferential

Edith Bunker character. She was an outspoken feminist. She had a husband at home, though.

Norman put two Black producers, Michael Moye and Bill Boulware, in charge of the writing and development of *227*, and initially I was happy about it. It made good sense, but the tables turned, you could say. Black people are not a monolith. We had differences, me and these two men.

They, for one, envisioned my character, Mary, as a single parent. While I, on the other hand, was committed to portraying a family that included a father and husband. I wanted to show a loving Black man as the head of a household. I wanted to bring some balance to the often-stereotypical portrayals of Black men as absent fathers or husbands—or mothers as estranged or deceased. The shows featuring Black characters were few enough, and single moms and dads were well represented. There was *Julia*, which starred Diahann Carroll as a nurse and a widow, raising a young son alone. Fred Sanford was a widower, living with a grown son, on *Sanford and Son*.

I had already, of course, played the single woman with no children and no man as Florence. Fans often questioned me: "Why did they not let you have a man over so many years?" The single thing and the single-parent thing had become negative stereotypes, and we Black people were tired it. Especially those of us who lived different realities. I happened, for instance, to have had a dad, whom I adored and who adored me and provided for me, complicated though that all may have been. So I was certainly not interested in further perpetuating the emasculation of Black men.

The character of my daughter, Brenda, was written negatively. They described her as someone who disliked other young people simply because they were breathing. I insisted that my daughter be a typical teen with friends and who had authentic and common teen experiences, like crushes on the neighborhood boy.

Our producer pair, Mike and Bill, were echoing positions and ideas that were in line with the desires and values of the network heads. They wanted my character, Mary, to be an owner of the building 227. I disagreed, feeling that Mary should be a fellow renter, which was actually consistent with the original stage play. My feeling again was grounded in wanting to be—and to represent—a central character who is on the same level as the other tenants, not their landlord or landlady. Our audience, I believed, might identify with my character dynamics more if they were on equal footing. The show was an opportunity to reflect most Americans who struggled every day to make ends meet. That's what I was about. My connection is always with the masses; I'm one of them.

I starred as Mary Jenkins, living in a building where she spends time sitting on milk crates on a large stoop, keeping company with her neighbors. There's her best friend, Rose.

There's Miss Pearl, who, rather than sit on the stoop, leans out her window with a pillow to cushion the sill. Our children, my husband, and other neighbors and visitors joined our conversations if they were not the subject. Their urban front porch in Washington, DC, was the center of the drama.

The cast included Hal Williams as my husband, and the young Regina King played our daughter. Both Hal and Regina had appeared in the stage production of *Two Twenty Seven*. So I told the producers we already had a chemistry that worked, plus Regina looked like she could be a daughter of Hal's. I fought for Regina, and she was fighting for the role as well. Several callbacks later, she won it! Alaina Reed Hall played Rose. Jackée Harry played our neighbor Sandra, who was as much a subject of the characters' talk as a part of it. Jackée played the femme fatale or, as our characters would rather call her, a floozy. She was Mary's nemesis, and the word on the street was that she was sleeping with the landlord. That is, until he died and left the building to Rose, much to everyone's surprise. Miss Pearl's grandson, Calvin, was played by Curtis Baldwin. When *227* was being developed, Dorian coached and managed Curtis and helped him land the role of Calvin. Dorian also wrote the script for an episode.

We shot the pilot and waited for NBC to make its final decision. They picked it up and positioned *227* behind *The Jeffersons*, because they figured the long-running show had one more season, and then they could move on seamlessly with *227*.

We got to a yes with the industry suits, but creative differences were soon to follow between me and the corporate gatekeepers. As meetings about all the matters continued, my heart sank more and more. Their agenda became apparent, and it conflicted with my own. It became clear to me that I had to speak up more loudly.

When it came to this idea that Mary Jenkins should be the owner of the building, I said, "I will not own the building under any circumstances. I will have a husband, and my daughter will have a father." I could not understand how two fellow Black people could reject my point of view. Michael made it appear that the network had the upper hand, but unbeknownst to me at the time, he had the authority. He could have honored my request. But he refused. I did get them to bend on the issue of Brenda's character. I myself was not willing to bend on that. That would have been too much. I was growing increasingly frustrated with these executives despite their impressive backgrounds.

Michael Moye had won a Norman Lear writing contest and was one of Norman's favorites. Bill Boulware was a successful writer on the show *Benson*. They had done great work before. But as players on my *227* team, they weren't compatible with me. I remember going home after the meetings feeling very down and dejected.

This called for a meeting with Norman Lear to iron out the differences. At this meeting Norman, Michael, and Andrew Susskind, the production manager, were present. I sat down, and Norman said, "Hi, Marla. How are you?"

"Fine," I answered. And we all know what it means when a woman answers "Fine."

"So, what's the matter?" he asked.

I wasted no time. "Andrew Susskind has been telling me that you all want this show to be exactly what I want. Well, it's not."

Michael sat up and said, "Marla has some things she wants, and there are some things I cannot accommodate her on."

I said, "Michael, why don't you tell us what those things are?"

"We don't see any need for the character Lester in the series, and the network wants your character to own the building." By this time I was feeling disrespected. This was a show that had come through me, and what I wanted was not being taken seriously. Michael was so confident in his demeanor that I got the gut feeling that a prior meeting had taken place without me.

"I am one of the have-nots; owning the building will make me one of the haves," I told Norman. "I don't know what that will do to my character, and I'm not willing to find out." I also told them all I felt the script was insulting to Black people, and I would not do it.

In this moment, at this meeting, I thanked Norman for

the years on *The Jeffersons* and said, "At this point in my life, I'd rather pick shit with the birds than do a show I don't believe in." I got up to leave, and Norman said, "Marla, wait, let's talk about what you want to do."

I answered. "Life is about men and women, not just women," I said in response to storylines that were too much about the women characters cat-fighting. The men, though, seemed to want that and believed in the entertainment value of that. The male character they imagined as a hero in the neighborhood was akin to the Hulk, who was a superhero known for his brute strength. Now, I have no issue with him at all. In fact, I had met the actor who played the man who turned into a big green mass of muscle to save the day. He was just great. But the character he played in *Hulk* was not what I had in mind for *227*. I wanted a male character who was a loving husband to Mary and a loving father to their daughter, Brenda. Not a stereotype or some mythical figure, but a portrayal of a real man, and one of good character. I wanted characters for our show who I loved, including the one that I played.

Norman then said something to me, in response to what was now open disagreement, that I wasn't quite expecting. "You know, I should have had you at the meeting at my house." He confirmed my instincts that there had been a prior meeting without me.

Norman turned to Michael and said, "Go talk to NBC, and tell them we're making some changes."

Michael replied, "I can't go tell them that."

But Norman was firm. "Tell them I said so—period." Michael left the table upset, but I didn't care. I was true to my vision and believed that it would serve a greater good.

The question of me playing a role on the show beyond acting came up because I felt strongly at this point that my input was going to be key to the show's success. Norm showed respect for my opinion but wasn't excited about the idea of me being a producer and a writer. "Writers stay up all night and write, and actors act." I told him I was willing to do that and everything else a producer did. I wasn't winning the argument. So I thanked Norman for the meeting and prepared to leave. The next person Norman was meeting walked up as I got myself together. Norman, interestingly, introduced me to this person as his "star." He may have intended it as a compliment, but I was not flattered. I left and called my attorney.

"Now I want to be an executive producer," I said.

Norman Lear was known for not allowing any actor to be an executive producer on the shows he developed. He was not singling me out. I heard Carroll O'Connor was also not given an executive producer title on *All in the Family* when he sought it. But I was determined to pursue a greater role on the show, because *227* was my baby as a producer. I had already succeeded with it onstage, and I now brought them an opportunity to make it a success on television. It was clear to me that the level of success I now pursued was not going to be easy—despite my prior successes. After the skirmish with Michael Moye, I knew that I was going to need to assume an executive producer role in order to make *227* become the best.

"I'll tell you right now, they're not going to let you do that," my lawyer said. I changed the subject and talked to him about going to Europe and singing.

He interrupted me. "Wait a minute, Marla. Okay, do you want to be an exec producer for the glamour or ego of it, or do you want to do the work?"

I replied, "I want to do the work!" He decided to have a talk with Norman's company.

After that, he came back to me and said that he'd gotten an agreement to grant me "all rights, courtesies, and privileges of an executive producer . . . without the on-screen credit." Another follow-up meeting was scheduled.

Norman himself didn't show up; rather, he sent a small team of men and women from his office, including Michael Moye and Bill Boulware. I got right to the point and asked Michael, "Did you do what Norman told you to do?"

To which he replied, "No, I didn't."

So, at this point, I was done with him, and I said, "I don't want you to do a goddamn thing on my show!" Everybody's mouths dropped open.

Michael said, "Well, I think I've been beaten up enough."

He walked out, and as he was leaving, I said, "Anybody else want to go with him?"

One of the guys in the room said, "Wait a minute. Bill is still here."

I looked at Bill, who was sitting there, and said, "Bill, do you want to work with me?"

He said, "I don't have anything against you."

I pointedly asked, "Do you think Black people want to see the show y'all wrote?"

Bill said, "I don't know what Black people want to see."

I asked, "Why not? You're Black, aren't you?"

The woman from Norman's camp said, "We want to hear what Marla wants."

For the first time, it felt like someone saw me . . . was on my side. It was certainly refreshing and empowering. What I later learned was that Norman had already told NBC they had locked me in to star in the show. After that meeting, the president of his company, Glenn Padnick, called me the next day and said, "I spoke with the network, and by the way, they are aware of everything that took place and told me that they didn't care. They were only interested in working with you."

With Michael gone, another executive producer was to join the production team. He had produced a successful sitcom and had a German partner he wanted to bring with him. Right away I let production know he couldn't bring his partner, because he had to work with Bill. I don't know if Bill ever knew that I had his back in that way. Although it was a rough beginning, things smoothed out some. And Michael Moye went on to co-create and executive produce *Married . . . with Children*, which had a very successful run. After *227*, Bill Boulware was part of the success of *The Fresh Prince of Bel-Air*. Both men were talented and found their lanes. I'm truly happy it worked out for them, and mostly I'm proud I trusted my intuition because *227* resonated with so many families of all colors across the country.

People were questioning me to my face. Ken Stump, who was the production manager, told me that if anyone came to me with questions, I should send them to him, and he would handle them. I said nothing, knowing I was going to do no such thing. Ken then attempted to fire the people I wanted for hair, makeup, and wardrobe, and hire who he wanted, without consulting me. I told him I had my choice over those departments. Ken said, "I believe that was the case, but things have changed."

I said, "Just a moment." I promptly phoned my attorney and said, "I'm sitting in Ken Stump's office, and he's telling me I don't have the right to decide who I want for hair, makeup, and wardrobe."

My attorney, Jake Bloom, asked, "Is he still sitting there?"

"Yeah," I replied.

He told me he would call me right back. We waited, and when my attorney called back, he told me, "I just called the office and gave them hell." He told me I had the choice of hair, makeup, and wardrobe. He spoke to Ken, and that was that. I met every obstacle head-on. Some of the actors did not know that I was an executive producer. They were not told. So they would attempt to go over my head when I made a decision. It was difficult at times, and sometimes downright hurtful, because they had no idea that I was in the background, fighting for them. You have to watch the battles you fight, because it doesn't always equal winning the war. Unbeknownst to me, though, I was walking an uncharted path. I was breaking barriers and making history in the industry for women and for people of color.

I was determined to present the kind of family and community most Black folks grew up with. We had an episode about homelessness, another about drugs and how young people could die using them, and another about Martin Luther King Jr. We had teenage storylines, like Brenda wanting to wear makeup too early (like my daughter, Angela), and defying our rules by sneaking out to a party and lying, and throwing a party in the penthouse that gets out of control. I was using my own experiences as a mother of teenagers, of events that were happening in the country and the world, just as I had on *The Jeffersons*.

I was lucky that I once again got to work on a set with good people and friends, such as Billy Dee Williams. This time the scene was an imagined sequence where we were all cast members of *Casablanca*. We had a ball, and Billy is always so great to work with. I later coupled up with him in a film called *The Visit*, where Hill Harper and Obba Babatundé played our sons. Rae Dawn Chong was also wonderful in it, along with Phylicia Rashad and Glynn Turman, who both always turn in meaningful performances. I'm very proud of that film, but unfortunately it didn't get the promotion it deserved. To this day I still consider Obba and Hill my sons.

Though *227* was a true labor of love, it was labor indeed. There were many battles I had to fight, and I'm sorry to say that some were with the cast. I starred in *227*, played a part in writing and producing, and I sang the theme song. Even though my voice is recognizable, many people didn't make the connection. None of that happened easily, though. As usual, the company had other ideas and other talent in mind to sing the theme.

The same thing had happened when I had the brief spin-off *Checking In*. Jazz pianist and good friend Horace Tapscott and I wrote the theme song, but we were told by the producers that they wanted someone who had experience writing for a TV show. Meaning, they wanted to hire their own friends. When we talked to the musicians who eventually were hired, we found out that it was their first attempt at writing for television. I realized then that I had been lied to. They offered to pay us for our version, but Horace said,

"No, we're not that hungry." In hindsight, we should have taken the money for the work we put in.

There was no distance between my community, family, and me as I climbed. Of course, I wanted to give them every outlet and opportunity I possibly could. This new show gave me another opportunity to do so.

Ray Colcord was brought in to write the *227* theme song, "There's No Place Like Home." I had created a song though with Monk Higgins that I preferred for the show. However, that idea was rejected. The producers rather asked me to sing lead vocals on "There's No Place Like Home." I don't know if they offered it to appease me or not. My daughter, Angela, and son Dorian did the backup vocals. Now I'm glad I did it.

We taped two shows a day for *227*, one in the afternoon and another in the evening, after dinner. We wouldn't have quite the same energy later in the day that we had earlier. Nonetheless, I noticed that the execs chose scenes from the evening show instead of selecting what was the best from both tapings. I don't know why. Maybe they were attempting to keep the process simple for themselves. I knew certain cast members had better scenes than the ones the execs were choosing. We had great and often better material in the first shows—when we were more rested—that went unused. I did join the editing meetings and ask who picked the scenes.

I've pushed the boundaries of my work description for nearly every job I've ever had, from working at Service

Bindery, at the Gotham Hotel, and later on at the theater. On the soundstages of television, it was the same thing. I like to get things done and do them well. Many times when I attended the meetings, someone said, "Marla, they need you on the set right now to run lines." I think it was in part to keep me out of the editing and decision-making processes.

I'd say, "I'm a fast study; I don't need to be there now."

Sometimes I'd designate Brenda Strange, my cousin, as a stand-in for myself so I was free to sit in on editing sessions. It was important for me to be there. I was the kind of producer who looked at everything because I wanted the best. Sometimes the writers complained because I cut out jokes that they thought were funny. My response was "You know what we're going to do for you? We're going to get the scissors, cut that joke out, give it to you, and you can take it home and keep it forever." After a while the writers would say the same thing to each other whenever one of them griped about something being deleted.

They'd look at me and say, "You know what we're going to do for him, Marla? We're going to get the scissors so he can cut the joke out, take it home, and keep it forever." We started having a lot of fun, and they started to see the value of having me in editing.

I made every effort not to push my weight around, despite being the star of the show. Whenever I had to make a decision, I'd ask myself, *What am I trying to accomplish?* or *Why am I doing this?* I also wanted to know the reasoning behind a cast member or producer not wanting to do something. I would step back and think about how their reasoning might make sense.

Some of the cast members, for example, would be frustrated because they only had four or five lines in a scene. At times they would get distracted when they thought the camera wasn't on them. So, after the run-through of each show, the director and I made it mandatory for the cast to meet with us in my dressing room to discuss these kinds of situations.

We would watch the run-through together, so that they could see when the camera was on them; that way, the actors who had few or no lines could see that if they stayed engaged, the camera could use their reactions, which were important to the scene. I was always looking at the bigger picture. My focus was the success of the show.

The show found its audience on primetime television. We had people's attention. They loved our characters. And the storyline evolved and changed, as they often do. I was generally happy with the show, but always open to what viewers were saying, what my fellow actors were saying, and what the other professionals we worked with were saying. We found agreement on some things and not on others over the years.

Hal Williams, who played my husband, Lester, complained that the producers talked to me all the time and wondered how come they couldn't talk to him. Not wanting to be confrontational, and since no one knew I was a functioning executive producer, I just told the producers to talk to Lester. But I was disappointed.

Hal—who, like me, began in community theater—was a comedic and dramatic actor who had played roles on *The Waltons*, *Roots: The Next Generations*, *Sanford and Son*, and the film *Private Benjamin* before *227*. I wanted to ask Hal at one point if he'd made the same complaints about Goldie Hawn when they worked on *Private Benjamin*.

When Jackée wanted to add a line, she went over my head to speak with the producers. They denied her at first, but as they saw the impact of her work, they began to say yes.

Jackée Harry was a New York City girl, a graduate of the city's High School of Music and Art. She became a brilliant comedic actor but began her training as an opera singer. After the High School of Music and Art, she attended Brooklyn Tech. She taught history there after graduating, and around that time she began studying acting at the renowned Henry Street Settlement in Manhattan's Lower East Side. She acted in her first play in 1973. It was written by Richard Wesley. She made her Broadway debut in *A Broadway Musical*. She came to *227* having only acted for television for a year, in a soap opera called *Another World*, opposite Morgan Freeman.

In the process of Jackée getting more lines, Alaina felt her character, Rose, was being diminished. She was right. Something like that impacts an actor's morale. Alaina appeared to be losing energy at work, and the network took notice. They considered letting her go. I reminded the producers, though, that Alaina was less impactful in scenes because they were allowing Sandra's character to sabotage her jokes. I asked them to give Alaina more to do and say, a chance to find her confidence again. Before *227*, Alaina Reed Hall was best known for playing Olivia, the kid sister of Gordon, on *Sesame Street*. She met actor Kevin Peter Hall on our show and married him on the show and in real life. They had two children together.

Helen Martin, who played Pearl, didn't see why she had the jokes they were giving her. Helen was an actress and writer known for *Death Wish*, a 1974 film about a man seeking revenge after his wife is murdered by street punks. Then later for *Don't Be a Menace to South Central While Drinking Your Juice in the Hood*, a parody of nineties films about the hood. And *Bulworth*, the Warren Beatty political satire film that also starred Halle Berry.

Curtis Baldwin played Pearl's son. He would later go on to work on other shows, like *Moesha*, another Black family situation comedy that was launched in 1989, and much more recently, he was on *A Black Lady Sketch Show*.

And my child Regina King, aka Brenda Jenkins, had her

own concerns about how her character was being portrayed. She didn't like the way Brenda dressed, because the kids she went to school with said she looked like a "doofus." I asked her if she wanted to be on the street with them or on the TV show. I reminded her that Brenda's character dressed that way because her mother made her. I told her we could even do an episode about it. I also advised her that if she got too grown, they would send her off to college, and she'd be off the show.

Regina was very smart and got it! In fact, she would come to me and say, "Does this look too grown?"

Regina, a native Angelean, is the daughter of a special education teacher and an electrician who early on supported her study of acting. They made it possible for her to be taught and coached for ten years by actor and coach Betty A. Bridges, before and during the run of *227*. Betty, the mother of actor Todd Bridges, worked with other successful actors, including Nia Long and Lamont Bentley. Her long list of Hollywood credits includes television series such as *Ally McBeal*, *The Practice*, *Moonlight*, and *NYPD Blue*.

There was a point during our show when everyone's hair got longer and wider by the episode. I remember thinking, *I don't want the show to be about hair*, so I cut mine off. Mary had a short Afro, and I ended up with fans complimenting my natural hair. I began to feel more connected to my community, but the producers didn't like it. They focused on the letters we received from two unhappy fans complaining that my hair was shorter than Lester's. I replied to both and told them I didn't think I should have to press and curl my hair or adhere to a European standard of beauty. Natural hair was beautiful to me. I asked them how they would feel if they were asked to make their hair look like ours. One wrote back and apologized.

I created the storyline for an episode about the Olympics, where my dear friend Willie Amakye, who was a four-time Olympic runner from Ghana, was highlighted. In that episode also starred the late Olympic gold medalist Flo Jo, who was a delight to work with, along with her husband, Al Joyner, and UCLA track coach John Smith. He is considered one of the world's top sprint and hurdle coaches. I loved the idea of using the show as a vehicle to pay tribute to the hundreds of athletes who train hard for four years and never receive anything.

Another show idea I introduced and cowrote featured my friend Veronica Redd as the mother of a drug dealer. Curtis's character, Calvin, gets caught up with this guy because he has money and looks successful. Even Brenda likes him. My character goes over to Veronica's house to tell her to watch her son, and she puts me out. During a community meeting in our building, Veronica's character shows up in tears because her son has been killed. We end up on her crying and saying, "What do I do? I have an eleven-year-old at home.

Somebody tell me what to do." I didn't want to squander the opportunity I had to tell stories that could make an impact. I truly hope I didn't.

Initially Jackée was cast for seven out of thirteen episodes and not more, because they thought her character was over-the-top. But her character, Sandra, became an audience favorite. The over-the-top-ness was the thing that made her portrayal of the character work. And Jackée ended up working every show and eventually became the breakout performer in her role, similar to what happened with me in the role of Florence on *The Jeffersons*.

At one point, I think what the network was looking for was a show between Mary and Sandra, without the family. They thought the bickering between them was the key to success. The thing is, though: Sandra's character didn't need Mary. And I told the network so. Jackée had transformed the character into her own brand, much like the persona created so successfully by Mae West. The persona was so strong, it didn't necessarily need an ensemble. She could do what she did with a mirror or alone, and it would still work.

There were seven cast members and twenty-two episodes in the first season. I assured each cast member they'd appear in every episode, so it wasn't like they were not going to be working. They'd be making money every week, but they had to know the show was not going to be about them exclusively. I had to run it down. I explained, "When it comes to somebody else's turn and they have the punch line, we support them."

I asked Jackée Harry to support Alaina Reed-Hall, who played Rose, in that way, and she replied, "You're asking me not to be funny."

I told her, "I'm not telling you not to be funny; I just don't want you to step on Rose's lines."

I knew that the reason Alaina had an attitude was because every time she had a joke, Jackée would add something extra to get a laugh just before Alaina could say her line, so Rose's lines were cut.

I fought for Alaina. I also took her to O. C. Smith's church, City of Angels, which practiced Science of Mind. I was hoping Alaina would hear some principles she could use to lift her spirits. I wanted our show, *227*, to win, and everyone on it to understand the importance of being a team, so I insisted that the cast come to my house for a meeting. I wanted to save the show and could see that without cast unity, we would be in trouble. The producers wanted to know why they couldn't come too. I reminded them that they had once told me they were too busy to deal with the problems we were having on the set. So I let them know, "I got this!"

During that cast meeting at my home, everyone finally came to a meeting of the minds. I gave everyone a breakdown of their roles. Helen, myself, the kids, and Jackée were on the show to get laughs. Hal and Alaina were the straight people who occasionally would get a laugh.

As the popularity of the show grew, so did stories about dissension between Jackée and me. Most of it was media hype, because negativity always sells. It just gave people something to talk about. The only squabbles we had were over the delivery of Jackée's lines. I understood Jackée wanted to be a star. She had performed in the soap opera *Another World*, but her dream was to be a headliner. And she was definitely good enough to be one. Funny, she wasn't the first choice for the role of Sandra—the network had wanted Sheryl Lee Ralph instead. I love Sheryl, but there was something magical about what Jackée had done in the room when she was auditioning. She originally came to read for the role of my sidekick, Rose. After her audition she asked if she could read for Sandra, and we said yes. Jackée was full-figured and reminded us of Mae West.

She was hysterical. She was ridiculous and funny. Even with that, the producers insisted that the network wanted Sheryl Lee Ralph. I explained to them that nobody would ever believe that Sheryl lived in the 227 building. She was so glamorous and had so much presence. I ended up convincing them that Jackée was our best bet. Sheryl went on to star in *It's a Living*.

I understood when the writers were writing more for the Sandra character than mine, because she was easy to write for and she was the femme fatale on our show. She brought something special to the varied expressions of femininity we had on the show with her gorgeous figure and legs. Each of us was beautiful and memorable in her own way. But Jackée looked like she was poured into her wardrobe. Male fans would comment to me, "That Sandra character with those hips . . ." They just loved her. I was thrilled to have Jackée on the show. I don't think she ever truly knew that. Fortunately we've worked together since on projects like *The First Family* and *Days of Our Lives*.

One of the best things about working on television was and is the people I had the pleasure of working with. After my family, they are the most important people in my life. Working together and getting to know each other over the years is a gift that keeps on giving. Helen Martin, who played the older woman known for talking to her neighbors through her front window, leaning on a pillow, was one of those wonderful people. Her straight, no chaser delivery on the show was hilarious. She was so gifted.

Helen was one of those people who refreshingly said what everyone else was only thinking, both on and off camera. The show took a poll of viewers and discovered that she was the most beloved *227* character among young people. She was one who—long after the show closed—remained my friend for life, until her passing in 2000. And the impact she made continues, long after she lived.

Helen supported the theater Angela and I started. Angela had a funny story to tell about how Helen lent her support—by way of a wad of cash in a brown paper bag. She pulled out the cash and said to Angela, "Count that. How much is it?" Then she pulled out another wad. "Count that. How much is that?" She continued doing this until Angela had counted out six thousand dollars.

Alaina and I also became very close. She was a well-known singer, and we performed together at my jazz club. I was there through her marriage to Kevin, until he made his transition, and when she was diagnosed with cancer. She fought hard, and I was constantly there supporting her and her new husband, Tamin. Jackée and I were at their wedding, as we had been for her wedding to Kevin. I still miss Alaina.

Hal and I will always be buddies. We check on each other from time to time, and he still calls me Mary, and I call him Lester.

Jackée ended up winning a well-deserved Emmy for her role as Sandra on *227*. I loved that we also got to work together on *Live in Front of a Studio Audience: Norman Lear's "All in the Family" and "The Jeffersons,"* produced by Norman Lear and Jimmy Kimmel in 2019. She was wonderful reprising the role of Diane. I later learned that Jackée and Jamie Foxx encouraged Norman to bring me back as Florence.

Then there is my bonus daughter, Regina King. Her journey to becoming the accomplished actor and director she is in our business has me in awe. I'm so proud of her. She still calls me Mom, and I embrace that. I was her mom on the set and a mentor behind the scenes. I'm gratified that she credits me with teaching her how to become a professional and have longevity in this business. Her talent is undeniable in front of and behind the camera. She deserves every accolade and already has at least four Emmys, an Oscar, a Golden Globe, eight NAACP Image Awards, and two Critics Choice Awards. She is a shining example of where listening, observing, believing, and trusting your instincts can lead you.

I've always found joy in seeing the young people around me try things, to be productive and creative—to express themselves in the arts and business. My youngest child, Dorian, cofounded and managed a great dance group called Body Language, which performed all over Los Angeles. Curtis Baldwin, Willie Reaves, and James Ellison were a part of it. My grandson Amil was also the youngest member. When the group performed at my nightclub, the boys brought the house down. Their popularity won them a spot at the closing ceremony of the 1984 Olympics with Lionel Richie.

Shows and projects have their run—some shorter, some longer. No matter what, you have to move forward, keep your life moving. In 1990, *227* was canceled.

Despite the show's success, we did not have the absolute support of the network. There was a constant struggle to agree on intentions and vision. As the talent, a woman, and a

Black person, I was limited by other people's ideas that I stay in my place as an entertainer and not be a decision-maker, a partner in the business of entertainment.

When I look back, I do have a few regrets. One of the biggest is when I won an NAACP Image Award for Outstanding Actress in a Comedy Series for *227*. During my acceptance speech, I neglected to acknowledge the writing staff, who were in attendance and had done a wonderful job. I was horrified. I wanted to make amends, so I took out a full-page ad in *The Hollywood Reporter* with my picture so they wouldn't miss it. I hope they saw it. I never wanted to disrespect or hurt anybody.

Some things that I am most proud of during the run of the show is that I insisted on having as many Black writers as we did white, including two Black women, Sara Finney-Johnson and Vida Spears. Both went on to executive produce on other shows.

Let me tell you how the Spirit works to get you where you want to go. A friend of my daughter's called and told her that this attorney wanted to give me some off-the-record advice. She was a Black woman who understood network politics and was offering to sit with me to share some information. So Angela and I met with her.

She said, "*227* is known as the show that will not die."

I couldn't understand and told her, "The fans love this show."

And she told me, "It was not the kind of family show the network or production company wanted to be connected to." I was floored and disappointed. But I also left that meeting feeling empowered and determined. This attorney did not have to share that information with me, but she was generous enough to have done so, and I appreciated it.

I regret that I didn't have the foresight to make sure that my daughter, Angela, who brought me the *Two Twenty Seven* play and produced it, received a business deal on the strength of our proven success—or, at the least, a formal partnership with me. Overwhelmed as I was fighting battles to sustain my career, I didn't have the awareness, knowledge, or capacity to fight for the interest of my beloveds. I missed some important opportunities. That attorney who had advised Angela and me in a private meeting at the time raised the important question: "Why is your daughter not on a lot right now with a deal?" She pointed out ways that I had "more power" than I realized. It's important to listen to good advice and questions. It's important to have knowledgeable, trustworthy people on your team. Don't miss the forest for the trees.

During the five years we did *227*, I fought for images, I fought for cast, I fought for good scripts, hair and makeup, wardrobe, and diversity in the writers' room. I had to fight the whole five years we had the show, but I'm happy to say that Glenn Padnick, the president of Norman Lear's company, always had my back. To this day we still care about each other. Although we had our share of disagreements, every time I saw Norman, he always gave me a hug and a kiss and said, "I love you."

And I told him, "I love you too." Because I did and still do.

There's a reason for everything—even if the reason is bad. Some truths are more difficult for us to uncover and digest than others. It took a while for me to realize that while my attorney received a verbal agreement with Norman Lear about me playing a producer/writer role, he never had Norman sign a written agreement to document it. And the show's producers were not told about me coming in as an exec producer. They were constantly asking, "Why is she doing this, and why is she doing that?" It seemed the only one who knew was me. They acted like I was trying to usurp their authority and take their jobs. But that didn't deter me. This has been the story of many women in film and television, as far back as Mary Pickford and Lucille Ball. We made a lot of progress when you look at the success of women such as Ava DuVernay, Shonda Rhimes, and my daughter, Angela. Women know how to get stuff done.

CHAPTER EIGHT

Vision and Loss in Leimert Park

I decided that it was time to sell: let it go completely. . . . People still come up to me all the time and ask when I am going to open another club. I tell them, "Watch my lips—NEVAH!!!"

The time had come for me to pivot from acting to other kinds of art and cultural work.

My dream was to build an entertainment center in the heart of our Black community that sort of modeled where I grew up. I was determined to create a place where Black culture could be shared and appreciated by Los Angeles and beyond. When I grew up in Chicago, the Jewish community had their area; there was a Greektown, a Germantown, and a Little Italy. Here in LA, there was Chinatown, Koreatown, and Little Tokyo. I envisioned the same thing for people from the African diaspora. I saw Crenshaw Boulevard . . . from Adams to Florence . . . could be the Black-owned part of town.

So, in 1990 I purchased a 1,200-seat theater in Leimert Park. I paid the Jehovah's Witnesses who owned it $3.2 million. I put down a payment of $500,000 with the intention to raise the rest from others and named it the Vision Theatre Complex. It sat smack-dab in the middle of the Leimert Park neighborhood, across from a small park and around the corner from an eclectic mix of shops—a block away sat Crenshaw Boulevard. The building had a lot of history. It was built in 1931 by multimillionaire Howard Hughes as a showcase theater for premieres. It stood three blocks away from our beloved PASLA. Angela's Crossroads Theatre group moved into the Vision Theater. It accommodated ninety-nine seats in the performance space.

We held acting classes for children and adults. We continued the Intensive Performance Arts Training (IPAT), an art camp that Angela started that was eventually funded by the City of LA with the help of then-Councilman Robert Farrell. One of our goals when we opened Crossroads was to build confidence in our youth, so that whether they became actors or not, they would know they had something to offer the world. Now that we were in Leimert Park, we connected our young students to different artisans who had shops in the community. When they graduated from the program, they could sell what they created.

Leimert Park began as a planned community in the late 1920s for low- to middle-income families. For the first twenty years or so, racially restrictive covenants kept Black residents out. This practice of exclusion was challenged but lasted until 1948, when the Supreme Court struck those kinds of laws and covenants down. It's about one and a half square miles in the Crenshaw district of Los Angeles. Black families moved in during the 1950s and redefined its culture. Now the area is about half Black, with Latinos making up about 25 percent of the population.

I chose Leimert Park because it was the perfect anchor, with its existing rich history of art, music, food, and Black culture being celebrated. There were already Black businesses up and down Crenshaw, ranging from dance studios and nightclubs to popular barbershops and restaurants. It put me in the mind of Black Wall Street. I wanted us to be owners again. This was the idea I wanted our people to embrace. It's the only way to control our community. Otherwise, we will always be subject to gentrification. I grew up watching it happen to my family and my neighborhood, and it's what's happening now down in Crenshaw and Inglewood. When I spoke about ownership instead of going nonprofit, this was what my goal was. I remember a person asking me, "Why don't you give the building to the city and let them take care of you?" I said, "Maybe God wants us to take care of ourselves." We've been given the intellect, the spending power, and unparalleled talent . . . Why are we always looking for someone else to take care of us? That means they will always be in control. It's why I owned the nightclub, Crossroads Arts Academy at 4310 Degnan, and the Vision Theatre. I was creating jobs, preserving jazz, and helping to build careers in the arts. I was also dedicated to creating a classy inner-city environment where our people would be proud to come to. I believe in ownership; I learned that from observing my mother and grandmother, and I still believe it is the game changer for our people.

I stepped out on faith, hoping that I could get Black celebrities, business owners, and investors to join me in making this vision a reality. I felt that after the Los Angeles riots was the perfect time, because property values had dropped and it was a buyer's market. I needed to raise three million dollars. My idea was that this would be possible if three million people gave one dollar, or one million people gave three dollars, or 120,000 people gave twenty-five dollars, and so on. Of course, this was before social media and crowdfunding platforms like GoFundMe existed. I remember that once the media came down to talk about what I was doing with the theater. I introduced them to the other business owners and took them to everybody's shops. My hope was that when we had events, the shops would stay open and reap the benefits of customers coming from the theater.

I was the largest supporter of the theater in the beginning, though. Angela had secured some funding through grants, but the goal was for the theater to pay for itself. Angela started counting heads and figured that if we just charged ten dollars per person, we could make some money and become self-sufficient. We could also pay the actors and director a stipend, so that everyone benefited from the community's support.

The program created for Crossroads was wonderful but got off to a slow start. I'm happy to say that once the community got wind that Crossroads was there, we became very successful. We had acting classes for children and adults, martial arts classes, dance classes, and voice classes. We gave scholarships to youth who needed them, and during the summer we had the IPAT.

We opened Crossroads, of course, to encourage and develop young talent. We started showcasing the talent we were developing with recitals. The space would be packed with parents, friends, and community supporters.

We produced several plays at Crossroads, including *Showgirls*, starring Peggy Blow and Lela Rochon, who made her stage debut with this performance. The play was directed by the late and prolific Cliff Roquemore, who would later couple with Angela's former college roommate Shay and father the beautiful and talented actress Xosha Roquemore. At one point, Crossroads Arts Academy was the place to be and was also the place Hollywood looked for talent. When Steven Spielberg was casting *The Color Purple*, his team looked at our students, and Jadili Johnson was cast as Celie's young son, Adam.

We had a great acting school. Whitman Mayo had his friend, legendary actress Beah Richards, come teach, and she was a gem. We were lucky. Beah Richards is as good as it gets when it comes to understanding theater language. She and Whitman were students of Frank Silvera's Theater of Being. I can't say enough how blessed we were to have her. Whitman also hired two other gifted actors, Wendy Raquel Robinson and Michele Richards. When I found out Wendy was at our school as both a student and later as a teacher, I was so proud. My great-grandchildren attended her school, the Amazing Grace Conservatory (AGC), and what they learned there has prepared them for a real career in the industry. AGC is responsible for producing actors at the top of their game, and Wendy, of course, is known for her great accomplishments and roles in the industry, including the hit television series *The Game*, where she played the momager of a professional athlete.

Wendy told me that it was our school, Crossroads, that inspired her to open her school, AGC.

That is why giving back is so important; you never know who will be inspired.

When we produced *Two Twenty Seven*, many of our students in the acting school earned roles in the play. Our goal was to give novices an opportunity to work with professionals. It was a perfect blend of community and professional artists. We had the likes of Badja Djola, Regina King, Art Evans, Hal Williams, Larry B. Scott, Nia Long, Christopher M. Brown, and Reynaldo Rey. All of our young students were great as well, and worth mentioning are Twyla Knapper, Sonya Winton, Willie Reaves, and Cynthia Howard. Cynthia, Sonya, and Willie would later guest-star on the TV show. Sonya, who later earned her PhD from Yale, is now Dr. Sonya Winton-Odamtten, a well-known television writer who, along with her partner, Jonathan Kidd, signed an overall deal with HBO. Both Sonya and Jonathan were executive producers of the hit series *Lovecraft Country*.

Cynthia and Twyla are both successful in business, and Twyla has remained very supportive of Susie's sons, Darnell and Darius. When Darius was ill with ALS, Twyla helped Angela, who was taking care of him, find him a great facility, and they were there with us to the end.

Rosie Lee Hooks, who was already a friend, was recommended by our director, Edmund Cambridge, to play the sexy Sandra role in the stage play. She was phenomenal in the role and eventually guest-starred in the show as Jackée's sister. Today Rosie balances her acting career with running the Watts Towers Arts Center, creating programming that powerfully impacts the Los Angeles community at large. Finally I must mention my good friend Amentha Dymally, who played the bougie tenant in the play. She is a consummate performer, and we were lucky to have her. Amentha also booked a guest-star role in the *227* TV show.

We were invited to move to the Inner City Cultural Center by its founder, Bernard Jackson.

As far as I know, Bernard was really the first one to coin the word "multicultural," long before it was a catchphrase for grants. Bernard had Asian, Black, and Latino artists who wrote, directed, and acted in plays that reflected their cultures. It was a wonderful time in the theater history of LA. Bernard touched the lives of so many; actors like Glynn Turman and Ted Lange got their start with him. He worked closely with Beah Richards and so many others who gave him accolades for showcasing their work and helping to launch their careers.

The next successful play we produced after *Two Twenty Seven* was *The Meeting*, written by Jeff Stetson and starring Dick Anthony Williams, Felton Perry, and Taurean Blacque. The play moved on to New York as a coproduction with Woodie King Jr. at his New Federal Theatre.

Woodie would bring Angela on to produce another play with him and Bernard Jackson called *Checkmates*, written by

Detroit's own Ron Milner. The play originally starred Denzel Washington, Paul Winfield, Gloria Edwards, and Rhetta Greene. Like *The Meeting*, *Checkmates* was a huge hit and played to sold-out houses. We eventually moved the play to the Westwood Playhouse. While we were preparing to open, we learned that Gloria Edwards was ill, so I took her role on in order to hold it until she came back. Gloria didn't make it back. It broke all of our hearts when she passed shortly after. When I had to leave, Roxie Roker took over the role, playing beside Ron O'Neal, who replaced Paul Winfield. Vanessa Williams, Bill Cobb, and Richard Lawson also starred in the play. *Checkmates* became such a hit that it eventually moved to Broadway. There, Denzel Washington and Paul Winfield were joined by the phenomenal Ruby Dee, along with Marsha Jackson, the cofounder of Atlanta's Jomandi Productions. The play was produced by Michael Harris and Hayward Collins. I worked together again with the playwright, Ron Milner, in another one of his stage plays, *One Monkey Don't Stop No Show*, along with Kim Fields.

In its heyday, the Vision served as a hub of sorts. The Nation of Islam minister Louis Farrakhan held a rally there to drum up support for the 1995 Million Man March. Hillary Rodham Clinton campaigned there. Poet Maya Angelou had a reading there, and a renowned healer conducted a wellness seminar at the Vision Theatre. We were also proud to premier *Lily in Winter*, starring Natalie Cole, along with

Jim Pickens Jr., Rae'Ven Larrymore Kelly, Salli Richardson, and me. *The Josephine Baker Story* was another film we premiered, starring Lynn Whitfield, along with Louis Gossett Jr. and Kene Holiday. It was great to premiere films starring Black actors in a Black community when our images were so often marginalized or nonexistent. It was important to me to create a venue where we could celebrate our work. The building served as a location for the film *A Thin Line Between Love and Hate*, starring Lynn Whitfield, Martin Lawrence, Regina King, and Bobby Brown.

I was in Bed Bath & Beyond when a young filmmaker came up to me with his mother. He said he had just gotten a three-picture deal and wanted to know if he could use my facility as a production office. That young man was John Singleton and his first movie was *Boyz n the Hood*.

My purpose in buying the Vision Theatre was to present the real history and greatness of Black people. I wanted to counteract the global images of our people that were negative and of our history as limited to slavery.

Tina Allen, who was a sculptress, was a very close friend. Sadly she passed away in 2008. But she was known for designing enormous sculptures of prominent historical Black figures. One that she created is a nine-foot bronze monument of author Alex Haley, which sits in Morningside Park in Knoxville, Tennessee. The monument to Haley has become a popular place for family photo opportunities. The figure of Haley holding an open book is big enough for visitors to sit in his lap along with the children gathered around him, also depicted in bronze. Tina Allen also designed a nine-foot bronze sculpture of labor leader A. Philip Randolph for a train station in Boston.

I wanted to use Tina's talents for a museum in the lobby. With plays, events, and movies running in the theater at night, I figured people could come during the day to see the museum—ten cents for children and twenty-five cents for adults.

Tina was to design a sculpture of the head of Ramses in the middle of the lobby, where a vent was located, so visitors walking under it would feel like he was breathing on them. Part of my vision was to also feature Akhenaten, one of the more famous pharaohs of Egypt.

When the organizers of the LA Festival rented out my property one year, I used that money to do upgrades. I had marble floors installed, along with a carpet that was designed with pyramids along the border. My plan was also to highlight the gods of ancient Egypt: Isis, Osiris, and Horus . . . the original trinity. I was going to hire Muslim men to serve as security at the Vision Theater. I had them at my club, and my customers loved them. They were respectful, and we always felt protected. I thought it would be powerful to have Muslim men interact with the visitors at the museum and teach them who Akhenaten was, as well as teach them the history of our people. That was my dream, but when I'd talk to people about this, I could see a shade slowly come down over their eyes—it was as if they were thinking, *What the hell is she talking about?* It never failed. Nobody ever got excited about this except Tina and me.

The museum experience was to also include films about the pharaohs and life in Egypt. It was my hope that the children in the neighborhood would see that Pharaoh Ramses looked like Leroy down the street. We always tell our youth that they come from kings and queens. Well, I wanted to show them, so they could physically see it. There would be documentary films showcasing the real history of African people, and I thought it was essential for our youth to know the story of their origins. To know how brilliant, beautiful, and bold their ancestors were. Also to explore what the transition was from being royalty to the slave trade. As they say, "If you don't know your history, you are doomed to repeat it." However, the bright side is, if you do know your greatness as kings and queens, you can also repeat that!

But like I said, Tina and I were among the few who understood the vision. Everyone else said, "How is this building going to pay for itself?" Looking back, I know now that visions take money—a lot of it—and back then I was slow to realize that most of the community leaders and business folks were not interested in helping. I was disappointed by that, because when they needed me, I was there.

One example is when a popular community leader, who will remain unnamed, had one of his big events, he asked me to see if Norman Lear would buy a table from him. I was also having an event at the same time for the Pan Afrikan Peoples Arkestra. Norman said he would only buy one table, mine or his. I said, "Buy the table from him, because it's a bigger organization and they've been there a long time." When I bought the theater, Whitman Mayo took me to that same leader to ask for help, and he gave me a flat-out no! It was heartbreaking.

I founded the Vision Theatre to take Crossroads to the next level. I imagined Leimert Park as a mecca for arts and artisans with the theater as the anchor. After a while we decided to expand our business and earn more income by opening a print shop. We saw it as a way to further support our community-based musicians, especially the Pan Afrikan Peoples Arkestra. We printed wedding invitations, brochures, posters, flyers, and the like and called it Hormar Press. Angela joined us in running the print shop.

I also wanted to create a jazz coffee shop. I went so far as to consult an architect. But he told me that the location wasn't good for what I envisioned. Close to the Los Angeles airport, the noise from planes overhead would cause problems.

Music, of course, was an important part of my agenda. Disco, funk, and R & B were the leading musical genres of the late 1970s and '80s. There were many wonderful artists—like

Stevie Wonder, Michael Jackson, Marvin Gaye, and many more—making great music that was at the top of the charts. Jazz and funk fusions were on the rise and even being played by former bebop musicians, such as Miles Davis. So much so that people in the music industry began to say that jazz as a music genre was dead. I grew up in Chicago in a time when jazz was our popular music—and danceable.

I wanted to offer what I enjoyed—acoustic music played in the style of authentic, classic jazz. The kind of music that lent itself to couples dancing. People weren't doing so much of that anymore either. They were dancing with each other but not touching. I wanted to give space to the musicians and vocalists playing the standards and big-band music in a relaxed and classy dining environment.

I was fine with all the new styles of dancing and playing, but I refused to accept the narrative that jazz was dead. No, classical Black music was alive and well in Los Angeles. We had locally based artists and those who came into town from elsewhere. I know because we gave them space to perform and rehearse.

I was thinking of the place as a jazz coffee shop when I ran into Larry Hearns, who owned the Memory Lane, an established and popular venue. His place featured performers such as Nat King Cole, Dinah Washington, Little Esther, and Lorez Alexandria. I told him what I wanted to do, and he talked me into buying his club. I loved the idea of carrying that tradition over into what I called Marla's Memory Lane.

The central idea was to showcase local jazz musicians. The Los Angeles scene was rich in those days; the national and world scenes were too, of course.

Horace Tapscott (you remember my great love, right?) was a leader in the musical and cultural communities and known to many as "Papa," which was the acronym for the organization he founded: the Pan Afrikan Peoples Arkestra (PAPA), also known as "The Ark." The Pan Afrikan Peoples Arkestra was originally called the Underground Musicians Association, established in 1961 by Horace with pianist Linda Hill and others in the aftermath of the Watts Rebellion in 1965.

A dear friend and mentor to me for close to eighteen years, Horace schooled me on the plights and challenges of jazz and jazz musicians. Horace took young musicians in their early teens and taught them to read and create compositions. Many of them went on to become successful and are still performing. Horace was "paying it forward," as they say, as a way of honoring the older musicians who embraced and mentored him as a teenager, like Gerald Wilson. Horace became an icon himself, recognized not only in his community but in Japan, Italy, Spain, and elsewhere in Europe and Asia. His beautiful wife, Cecilia, was an avid community volunteer whom I was proud to call my friend. They had a daughter,

Renee, and son-in-law, Micheal Wilcots, who went on to take care of her father's archives.

Together we brought in the best of the best to Marla's Memory Lane, including contemporary hitmakers such as George Bohanon, Gil Scott-Heron, and Patrice Rushen. We featured Ernie Andrews, Gerald Wiggins, Monk Higgins, Ndugu Chancler, Oscar Brashear—the list is long.

The great Dizzy Gillespie. Etta James and Eddie "Cleanhead" Vinson recorded their Grammy-nominated album *Blues in the Night, Vol. 1: The Early Show* live at Marla's Memory Lane. We featured Hank Crawford and other legends from around the country, like Bobby Hutcherson, Jimmy and Jeannie Cheatham, O. C. Smith, Larry Gales, Vi Redd, Kenny Burrell, Jimmy Smith, Mercer Ellington, Freddie Hubbard, Gerald Wilson, Ahmad Jamal, Willie Bobo, and more. At one point, I was credited with hiring the most jazz musicians in the city. That made me smile from ear to ear.

The restaurant aspect of Marla's Memory Lane was also inspired by two ladies who visited Crossroads Theatre and asked me if I knew of a nice place in the Black community where they could bring their friends from out of town to have dinner. I couldn't name one place at that time. There were nice restaurants in the marina. I realized we had nothing like that in our community.

So, Marla's Memory Lane became a jazz supper club where people could experience fine dining, live music, champagne, Sunday brunch, and, of course, where they could have their own celebrations. We didn't limit ourselves to one or two categories and functions. Monday night was blues night, and some of the top blues artists would perform. We even had a magic show for children.

My grandson Amil got his first job at the ripe old age of six years old when he hosted the magic show, and eventually he graduated to performing magic with his mentors, our headliners, the Amazing Mayseo and Dorian the Magician (not my son).

Marla's Memory Lane, I'm so proud to say, became the club where people from all over LA would come for great food and great live music by innovative artists. Our reputation brought tourists, and of course, me being on *The Jeffersons* didn't hurt.

Owning a jazz club gave me an opportunity to pursue my first artist love again and find the courage to sing in front of an audience. I was so at ease acting, but singing made me feel vulnerable in ways that acting did not. I had to work up to it. One way of doing that was to take singing lessons. I was introduced to Roger Love, who taught Seth Riggs, and I started going to him regularly. I witnessed my voice get stronger and the range increase. Roger is a fantastic coach. Not only does he know how to expand voice range, but he also gives you a healthy dose of confidence. I was fortunate, because the musicians were always so encouraging, especially Kenny Burrell and Larry Gales.

First I started singing a song here and there during Sunday brunch with Larry Gales. Finally I did my own show, and it went well. I was privileged to do another show with my dear friend Ernie Andrews, and we had a great time singing "Time After Time" together.

I mostly chose songs that were made popular by some of my favorite artists. My repertoire included "Wave" by Antônio Carlos Jobim; "Promise Me," a song that Sarah Vaughan made popular; "Easy Living," sung by Billie Holiday; and finally Dinah Washington's "What a Difference a Day Makes." I loved ballads—Brazilian and Latin music as well. Whenever I did a show, Gerald Wiggins (The Wig) would come play with me, along with his band.

Our comedy shows were great too, thanks to Reynaldo Rey—who famously performed in the film *Harlem Nights*, and who many may not know wrote for Redd Foxx. Lewis Dix debuted there, and so did the brilliant Robin Harris, who became a standout for his role in the Spike Lee film *Do the Right Thing*. At the time he was a waiter who asked me if he could showcase his comedy act. I said yes, and he was great and went on to become a legend among comedians. He passed away way too soon.

D. L. Hughley appeared at our place long before he became one of the Kings of Comedy. I had no idea at all who he was. And he didn't know enough about me to know that I didn't tolerate cursing from the stage. He came in one evening, got up to perform, and did indeed spit out a cuss word or few, and you could hear the audience start mumbling "Ohhhh," and start looking for me. Everybody knew I didn't like foul language, but he hadn't gotten the memo. I walked right up to D.L. and interrupted his set, applauding as I went. I walked him off the stage and said, "Young man, come back when you have some clean material." To this day D.L. jokes about this and says, "Am I glad I didn't listen to you!" When he got his television show *The Hughleys*, he invited me to play the role of his mother. When I saw him in the casting office, he brought back the memory and said, "I worked your club once." I said, "You can work there again if you are clean." I had a ball working with D.L. and the rest of the wonderful cast on his show. I love him, and he always looks after me when he sees me out and about.

Besides creating a jazz experience for the LA community, I facilitated the training of servers and waiters. It was important to me to support the community by helping our people learn marketable skills. I wanted our folks to understand how to give good service. I promoted what I valued, including the importance of taking pride in work and service. I wanted our servers to be able to go further and secure jobs at other top restaurants if they so chose.

Finding an experienced manager who understood how to run a multifaceted club like Marla's Memory Lane was particularly tough. But it was necessary. When people see you on TV, they assume you are rich and don't need any help. It was hard, and I spent a lot to make the club something the community would be proud of. And I must say, there were times when it was certainly rewarding, especially when I got to employ noted jazz musicians and watch how audiences came to support their music in their neighborhood. Often we would be packed! I would work on *The Jeffersons* by day, and I worked at the club at night.

Burning the candle at both ends that way and running a business that way were not sustainable. I thought I would always be running the club. We had a good eighteen-year run. But the neighborhood and local music scene changed in ways brought on by the progress our country made away from legal racial segregation. White music fans had long slipped into venues in segregated Black places. But now more jazz clubs were popping up in white communities. It appeared that jazz was not as dead as people had been saying after all. Black music lovers started going to the jazz clubs in white-run venues too—the ones they couldn't go to before in neighborhoods where they had not been welcomed.

There were those who promoted the idea of Black people supporting Black businesses as a way of balancing the scales of what we'd lost and gained with racial integration. But that movement did not catch on soon enough to save our club. There were fans who would come to my club during the Sunday champagne brunch because the word was that

I was always there. My *Jeffersons* fame helped a bit. I liked to greet people and make sure everyone was having a good time. So I was fine with it. What I didn't like so much was when fans would ask me to come outside to take my picture but would then take their business elsewhere. I'd ask if they were coming into our place for brunch, and they'd say they had reservations in Marina del Rey. I don't think it even registered how hurtful that was to me.

We set up retirement plans for our employees and had Bank of America come in and talk to them about saving for their futures. In fact, B of A offered to give each employee twenty-five dollars when they opened an account.

I looked at my glass as half full, not half empty: Crossroads Arts Academy, our community theater company, was a success. It did benefit others, and I am proud of that. I still have parents who come to me and say, "My child went to your school, and now they're doing so well." I learned a lot, including about myself: my strengths, and my weaknesses. I'm grateful that I did take the opportunity to apologize to Shay, who played such a pivotal role in our success and didn't deserve my rudeness when I was missing the attention of my daughter.

I will always remember with pride what Angela, Shay, and all of us did in our work to advance the arts and culture in our communities, and especially how the show *227* came out of our community theater.

We produced good plays over the years and received

great reviews. God is awesome. But running a nightclub was hard. While having the platform and notoriety that I had helped business, there were ways in which celebrity made the work of successfully running the business harder. I was warned about going into the nightclub business, because so much cash changes hands that it's easy for money to be mishandled—as in, disappear. When Jimmy Smith came to perform at my club, his wife, Lola, tried to give me some pointers.

I still had Marla's Memory Lane, which wasn't making much money anymore, and now I also had the Vision Theatre. By 1990 I owned three-quarters of the commercial property in the neighborhood. Somehow I kept everything afloat for seven more years.

We could've shown our community as a thriving area, but instead most of the shops closed. When I was losing the building, I had a plan to do a big event for Christmas. I went to the councilman to request a street closure so that a sleigh could take people up and down the street to the different shops. Unbeknownst to me, some of the shop owners had already spoken against it. I went to some of the shop owners and asked them, "What is it I'm doing wrong? I can change it." I didn't get an answer, but I did feel unwelcomed.

I don't know if I was getting too much credit because I was a celebrity or because I had too many ideas . . . Whatever it was, I found myself feeling alone with a vision that very few seemed to be on board with. There was a pastor who told me he was trying to gather support from other pastors to help me save the building, but he said a prominent pastor told him that he was hoping I'd lose the building, because he was trying to get his money together to purchase it. That was disheartening.

There was another one who said that "a woman didn't need to own all that property."

I must acknowledge some of those who did step up and help me, like Oprah Winfrey, who wrote a check for $25,000. In my devastation, I don't think I ever properly thanked her . . . THANK YOU SO MUCH, OPRAH.

A talk show host in New York, whose name I regret I can't recall, spoke about me losing the building, and I started receiving checks from folks in New York. THANK YOU! And thanks to Whitman Mayo for speaking to Bill Burke, president of the LA Marathon, on my behalf. Mr. Burke gave a generous donation of $100,000 when I was purchasing the building. I was so moved by all of the people, coast to coast, who contributed. I would be remiss if I didn't thank my dear friends Maxine Waters and Diane Watson, who have always advocated on my behalf.

There were people in the community who didn't really have the means but insisted on donating anyway. It warmed my heart. There was an older man who reached into his pocket to give me a dollar. I remember a woman who walked up to me in the bank, gave me twenty dollars, and said, "I love you. Thanks." Another woman gave me twenty dollars every time she got her check. When I think about those people, I wish I could have hugged and connected with them more. I was buried with the problems that came with trying to save the building. I didn't have time to just be in the community.

The theater fell on hard times after the 1992 uprising resulting from the Rodney King beating and subsequent not-guilty verdict. With our community residents hurt and distracted, we needed people from outside of our community to come and support us. But that just didn't happen.

I struggled for five more years, until 1997, before I lost the complex in June 1997, after a fundraising effort failed to raise the $250,000 bank debt. I think about that last-ditch effort I made to save it. I had blinders on at that point and wasn't listening to any advice.

I gathered up $50,000 to give to the bank, but my attorney told me not to give it to them. I wanted the bank to see that I was really trying, so I ignored him and gave the money to them anyway . . . He was right. They took the money and then took the building. Over the years I spent about $2.5 million on the complex.

The city started enforcing an earthquake code, and it was too costly to make the improvements, so I sold the building to then-Councilman Mark Ridley Thomas, who is now one of our LA County supervisors. Sometimes you just have to let it go, take your hands off. I thought I was running a marathon, but I was wrong. I was in a relay race, and it was time to pass the baton. I wasn't supposed to be there.

When I lost the property, the new bank representative said, "If I had been here, I would never have taken this building from you. We don't know what to do with this property. You're the only one who had a vision for it. Now that the city has it, they are going through the same thing you did . . . trying to figure out how they're going to save it and what they're going to do with it." It was hard on me when I lost the theater. I worked hard, but it wasn't enough. I came to grips with that. When I was locking the door for the last time, I looked up and asked God, "Why? I don't understand." I heard a voice say, "There's no vision here." I accepted that, locked the door, walked away, and never looked back. I had a vision, but you can't have a vision for somebody else. They have to have a vision too. And sometimes you don't know how God is using you. So many people have given me recognition and awards for putting my money in the community. From local residents, to politicians, to gang members. They come up to me and say, "Thank you for what you tried to do in our community."

I didn't have a choice when it was time to close the club down. The image of the doors locked to me for the last time is forever lodged in my memory. It was around Father's Day, 1999, and I'd gone to see Ruby Dee's wonderful performance in a one-woman show. After the show I invited her to come to the club, and she did. Thing was, my cook hadn't shown up to work. I had to cook most of the food myself. I was embarrassed, to say the least. But the food was good enough that I gave Ruby the leftover food to take back to the cast. Such was my last act in Marla's Memory Lane. I closed the doors that day, and that was that.

I leased the space out a couple of times, but the club managers also had a hard time keeping it open. When I went there to dine myself, it hit home to me that the quality of service had gone down. And it occurred to me that this would have an adverse effect on my reputation—even though I wasn't running the place anymore. I decided that it was time to sell: let it go completely. My customers, like me, missed the place. Even if support for the place had diminished over time. People still come up to me all the time and ask when I am going to open another club. I tell them, "Watch my lips—NEVAH!!!"

They say, "I miss it, though."

And I say, "I miss it too, but I don't miss paying for it."

Encouraging and celebrating local talent and Black talent and service to the community were important to me. So I started the Concerned Helpers of Inner Community Endeavors (CHOICE) Awards. I brought on my cousin Sharon Graine to help me launch it.

CHOICE raised funds by producing events, which included fashion shows, dinners, and tributes to jazz luminaries. Musicians would perform, and I got a chance to sing. Sharon had experience with fashion shows and taught those who were not models how to walk and present the clothes. We featured top local designers like Linda Stokes, Queen Ahneva Ahneva, and Peter Lai. We had top models like Toi and Kathy Arnold, Carla Kendall, Melvin Taylor, and Kathleen Bradley-Overton, aka Mrs. Parker from Ice Cube's Friday franchise. Kathleen actually went on from the CHOICE Awards to become the first Black female Barker Beauty for *The Price Is Right*.

We would choose two organizations each year to give money to: one dealing with youth and one dealing with adults. We were able to give money to charities that helped with domestic violence, recovering addicts, and the homeless, and we gave to the Boys & Girls Clubs and charities that give scholarships to youth. We also gave to Reverend Bean, who had an AIDS foundation, and we were the first organization to support him.

You could find Errol Collier ("Sauti," we called him then) backstage during the entire CHOICE function, counting money. He was my accountant during my time at *The Jeffersons*, Marla's Memory Lane, and the CHOICE Awards. My family grew close to him, his wife, and his two daughters. Like us, he believed in investing in and supporting community organizations and businesses.

He helped us to know exactly how much we raised and

were giving to the organization we were funding that year. We always announced what we made to the audience at the end of the evening. And we always sold out. We ran CHOICE for nearly ten years. My dear friend Virginia Higgins Bland came on board our fourth year as an organizer and host. I'm very proud of the work we did and the huge success we had.

After I locked the doors for the last time, I would drive by the Vision Theatre, and it was as if I had never been there. I didn't have any feelings about all the work we did. I thought, *God is awesome! He's taken me right by here, and I feel no connection with a place I was at for almost ten years.* There was a huge weight lifted from my shoulders that I didn't even know I'd been carrying. We think sometimes we are supposed to be someplace we want to be, but if it's not God's plan for us, no matter what we do, it's not going to work.

I've had a lot of time to reflect on the building and even my nightclub. When I was able to understand my relationship with trust and money, I realized it was inevitable that I would eventually have to walk away from both businesses.

It makes me think about Nipsey Hussle and what he'd been doing. What a tremendous loss. His efforts to build up the community were exactly what I was doing with Crossroads, Vision, and Marla's Memory Lane. I am proud of the generations that have come behind me who understand the value of building up our community. Nipsey was an entrepreneur whose vision not only empowered his family through business ownership but supported and encouraged other Black people to become business owners as well. Nipsey created jobs and started an organization called Vector 90, where youth were educated in science, engineering technology, and math.

I must insert here that my daughter had the vision for Crossroads Arts Academy and Theatre, and that seed grew into a place where youth and adults flourished. She was smart enough to use my celebrity brand and my money. We laugh now at how clever she was, manipulating me so when she was young. But she is a visionary, a community organizer who puts in the hard work required to nurture our communities and our culture.

Toward the end of my effort to save the Vision Theatre, I may have stepped on some toes or rubbed some folks the wrong way. For that I sincerely apologize. I say this because, while I have some friendships that are strong to this day, there are a handful of people I feel estranged from. After I lost the building, I was devastated, and this caused me to retreat. Sometime after I closed the theater down, I attended a workshop with a spiritual coach named Al Joy.

He said to me about the Vision, "Just to think, you did all this for love—the love you didn't get as a little girl." Of course, I didn't get what he was saying then. But now I understand. A little late, but then again . . . it's never too late.

CHAPTER NINE

Always Listen to the Spirit

When God leads you to do the seemingly impossible, the worst thing you can do is shake your head and say, "No. No way, Lord. It won't work." That shows no confidence in God, which translates into no confidence in yourself.

By the mid-1980s, I was blessed, and I had made a nice home for my family in Inglewood, California. But I was also now ready for something else—a dream house, a home with a view. I moved my family to Los Feliz, which sits between Hollywood and Silver Lake. It's known as the birthplace of Walt Disney Studios.

I found one house there that was nice, but it had a driveway that required me to back out of it, and that proved to be cumbersome. So I looked for another one. I prayed for a circular driveway and a pool to go along with a view.

Before long my Realtor believed he'd found the house with it all. The driveway was not only circular but big enough to fit ten cars. It had great closets, with windows with views of the city. I was initially hesitant to look at it. But I thought it was a pretty house, nestled as it was on a hillside. So I did a walk-through. The property included a big guesthouse. Each of the four bedrooms in the main house had its own bathroom.

I was able to get a good deal because the previous owner of the home had defaulted on the loan. But that same previous owner did not go out without a fight. At one point, he locked himself in one of the bedrooms. I'm told that he had to be dragged out of the house. By the end of the matter, he was able to strip the home of its plumbing. He gutted the kitchen, even took the sink.

Soon after we moved in, I got a knock on the door, and famed interior designer Warren Sheets was standing there. I didn't know who he was at the time. Warren said, "We were trying to do some work for the former owner, and we'd love to show you what we wanted to do."

"If you don't mind hearing 'NO' a lot, you can come on in," I said. He came in, and from that moment, Warren and I forged a friendship and a winning working relationship that have lasted to this day.

African art is a passion of mine, and Warren knew how to incorporate what I collected into the design. Working with a licensed interior designer gave me access to the showrooms on Melrose Avenue in Los Angeles that catered to the trade. Then I met a man who had returned from South Africa with unique art and furniture. I found out he had a whole storage facility full of stuff. I bought chairs and masks from him. We even found a woman who did carvings into carpets. Warren met an artist who did glass etching on Robertson, and they carved a figure of me into it. It's gorgeous, and when I eventually moved, I took it with me.

I had lovely neighbors there, including Richard Thomas, who played John-Boy on *The Waltons*, and his wife Alma. They lived across the street. We became friends. I hosted parties. I threw a fortieth birthday party for Berlinda Tolbert, who'd worked with me on *The Jeffersons*. And even Nina Simone came to dinner. And I threw a surprise party for my grandson Amil. Natalie Cole brought her son, Rosie Lee Hooks brought her son, Beverly Todd brought hers as well . . . and there were so many others who brought their families. It made my heart full to see people enjoying the property. We even had Mayseo the magician come and perform. He made his dramatic entrance to the theme song from *2001: A Space Odyssey*, and the kids were in awe—that is, until they swarmed him, trying to figure out where the dove had disappeared to. They were looking inside his tuxedo and checking his magic boxes. It got so bad that Mayseo grabbed his stuff and made a run for it to the pool house.

I couldn't believe I owned such a marvelous house. And the best part became the sunroom. It's where I had breakfast while I looked out over the grounds. It reminded me that God was in charge. But while I loved the place, it was not to be our forever home. While Angela and I were having cups of tea, enjoying the view of the city one day, I heard Spirit say, "It's time to go." I said to Angela, "God has been good. He has given me so much more than I ever imagined. But they're messing with me on *227*, and I got the feeling it might end. I'm not going to kiss no ass for no house. I think I'm going to sell it." And that's exactly what I did.

I put my dream home up for sale, and I got more than I paid for it. I had said to God, "If it's time for me to go, send me the buyer, and I'll sell the house." One thing I won't do is allow a material possession to own my heart or my wallet. Good thing I sold, because *227*, once referred to as the show that wouldn't die, did die. When I sold the house, that was the same feeling I had when I left Buddy. My friends told me, "I wouldn't leave my house if I were you," but it's just a house.

God has blessed me with six houses since then.

Every step of the way, I've learned how to live. And one

of the greatest lessons I've learned is that you can't be envious of other people's gifts. What they do or don't have has nothing to do with you. And what's good for them may not turn out so well for you.

My daughter introduced me and the family to the world-renowned herbalist Dr. Sebi. He was one of the brilliant people that I've been blessed to know, and he helped me take care of my health. Chile, at his recommendation, my sister Susie and I took some mushrooms. The idea was to allow what blocked us to fall away and to gain insight that would free us to be more of ourselves. Initially Susie was the only one who was going to take them. I agreed to pick up some that he was preparing for her. I went to his house to get them, and I asked him, "How come you didn't prepare some for me?"

Sebi said, "You want some?"

I said, "Yeah!" He gave me enough for both of us.

When I got home, I rushed upstairs to the bathroom, and while still in there, I decided to try some of the mushrooms. Well, shortly afterward, I looked in the mirror. My face was swirling and twisting around . . . It looked like a monster. Don't judge me, but you know that saying "Misery loves company"? Well, so does tripping!

I immediately went to Susie and said, "You need to take yours too." I knew I could not do this alone.

The Jeffersons was on the television, and I started talking to George and Weezy on the screen as if they were in the room with us. When Susie saw me talking to the TV, she got scared. The mushrooms were making me laugh, but they were making Susie paranoid. The more tickled I got, the more afraid she became, and poor Susie eventually had to leave me and go upstairs. My daughter says I left a message on her answering machine around 6:00 a.m. I was laughing so hard, I could barely speak. I managed to say, "We took some mushrooms."

Angela said Susie was in the background, screaming over and over, "Help us, Angela!"

My daughter came over and made us some oatmeal and peppermint tea. She said we needed to eat in order to start coming down, and she stayed with us until we were able to calm down. Susie was pacing and shaking her head. She told Angela, "If I see that muthafucka Sebi, I'm gonna kill him!" Sebi told us that mushrooms take you within. We went within, all right . . . Chile, we went all the way in somewhere. I just don't know where the hell it was. We still laugh about that to this day.

Some of my family members do partake in plant medicine, and they do so with real shamans. So I'm not against it. But I wouldn't suggest anyone taking mushrooms without a professional guide. In all seriousness, I had envied what I thought was special treatment Susie was receiving from someone we respect, and I didn't want to be left out.

Just a thought on envy: When you envy other people and

what they have, you're apt to make a wrong decision. It also puts you in the position of comparing yourself to others, and this takes your focus off your intentions. Envy also puts you in a low vibration emotionally. It feels bad and shows that you're thinking from a place of lack, based on what you don't have. The Universe has a unique way of delivering your good to you in perfect time; now, the key is, it is done to you as you believe, so it's a faith walk. You can't receive someone else's blessings, and you have no idea what that person's life journey is about, so stay on course and know your good is coming. What is meant for you will come.

Over the years I have acquired so much, in riches and recognition, and I must say, I've enjoyed it. But no blessing is greater than mental and physical wellness. Health really is our wealth. We are so conditioned to work hard and "get the bag," as my grandson Amil would say, that we often forget to balance our grind with self-care. We underestimate the critical role sleep and relaxation play in helping us to reset.

I didn't always practice what I now preach. I was raised in a place where and a time when none of this was talked about. I loved candy, for example. One of my favorite things to do as a kid was to buy a big dill pickle and put a peppermint stick in it. When I became an adult, I fell in love with Snickers bars. I started smoking when I was eighteen, mainly because I wanted to blow smoke rings and French inhale like I saw the movie stars do. I was shy, so whenever I went somewhere, I would smoke so I wouldn't have to look at people. I smoked for years, and one day I gave myself a date to quit. I told myself with every cigarette that "it's okay to smoke, because on this date, I'm going to quit." I guess I programmed my brain, because when that time came, I quit and never went back. That was over sixty years ago, I'm happy to say.

Our temple is our vehicle, and like with a vehicle, we need to put good fuel in it. We have to take care of the inside even more than we tend to the outside. That means eating healthy food, drinking lots of water, and holding good thoughts . . . Mind, body, and soul create the wholeness we need to not only reach success but also to sustain it.

I learned the value of having a healthy body and mind as a baseline when my real health challenges began and recovery became the name of the game.

In 1996 Reverend Wonders, a pastor from out of state, asked me to record a promotional video for his church. I agreed but told him I had to run to the bank first. I drove into the parking lot of Bank of America and waited for someone to pull out of a space. I got impatient because they were taking forever, so I pulled into another space, where I was forced to walk around two concrete structures and a high curb. What happened next is why they say "Patience is a virtue"! I tripped on the curb and fell into the street. I was holding something in both my hands and fell so fast, I couldn't stop myself, and I landed on my face!

The security guard ran over to help me get to the bank, but I said, "Please take me back to my car." I was embarrassed, and even more so, I was upset with God. Inside the car we had a fight—or at least I had one. I said, "What are you doing? You let me fall, and I'm hurt."

I waited for an answer, but all I heard was "You better get in the bank before it closes."

Once inside, the person in front of me took one look and said, "You can take my place." I had no idea how crazy I looked.

Maybe because I was in shock, or embarrassed, or just determined to get to my next appointment . . . but it never occurred to me to look in the rearview mirror. I didn't look at myself until I got to the Vision Theatre. I went into the bathroom, and I was a mess. My lip was swollen, and there was blood on my forehead. I tried to wash my face with the pretty pink soap we had placed in the bathrooms, and my face was immediately on fire. My skin was raw and bruised. No wonder the person at the bank had let me go first. I went around the corner to meet the pastor and tell him what happened and that I wouldn't be able to do the interview. Would you believe he asked me to do it anyway? And would you believe that I did it? I don't know what I was thinking; I was either in people-pleasing mode, or in shock, or both. While filming the interview and dabbing the blood off my lips, I said, "In case you're wondering why I'm sitting here, looking like a fool, I fell!" What I was thinking but didn't say was *Why does this pastor still want me to do this interview looking the way I look?* And I had a question for God as well: "Why did you let me fall?"

After the interview I decided I was going to wait to go to the hospital, because I knew they were going to keep me and I still had some other things to do. I was very lucky, because once I got there and they took my blood pressure, I learned it was three hundred over two hundred. Even after that, I still didn't take any blood pressure pills.

My next incident happened in 1997. I was scheduled to film a commercial in the Valley, on Ventura Boulevard, but I was late, so I decided to stop somewhere and call them. I spotted a phone booth in a little strip mall and parked my car next to some gravel.

I started across the gravel, and I must have blacked out, because the next thing I knew, I was on my face again. A man was on the telephone, and I asked him if he could call my agent to let the commercial team know I was going to be late. As I gave him the number, there was an elderly lady behind me who kept saying, "Lie down! You're bleeding. Lie down!"

The man informed me that he called my agent as well as the paramedics. And then he said, "The paramedics told me, whatever she does, don't tell her to lie down." That shut the lady up.

When the paramedics arrived, one of them was very attentive to me. She asked my name, what day it was, and where I was, and then took my blood pressure. When she asked me how old I was, I told her thirty. She probably thought I was tripping. She took my blood pressure on my left arm, then, without saying a word, she took it on my right arm. The paramedic looked at me and said, "I thought something was wrong with the monitor; that's why I took it on the other arm. Your blood pressure is three hundred over two hundred."

I looked at her and said, "I know. I have to go to the hospital."

She told me, "Well, there's one right nearby, so we'll take your car over there and park it in case they keep you." I was relieved. I stayed there until they brought my blood pressure down. I went to the bathroom to assess my injuries—my nose was fine, but everything else was red. Once I left , I decided to stop by the commercial shoot.

When they saw me on set, they said, "Oh, no, no. You didn't have to come."

I headed home and on the drive there, I said to God out loud, "Okay, you keep knocking me on my face, and it hurts, so I promise I'm going to check this out and do something about my blood pressure."

I checked myself into a hospital again. I wanted to know what was causing my blood pressure to be so high. The battery of tests they put me through was inconclusive, and the doctors disagreed with each other on the cause. I was left disillusioned. The irony, however, is that the same hospital would later be the one that saved my life.

Lee Meriwether had invited me out to see her and Lloyd Bridges in the play *Love Letters*. Lee and I had met a month earlier in a makeup room while getting ready for our interviews at an independent television station. Before the play started, I decided to go to the restroom. I leaned over to flush the toilet, and I felt something go "bloop" in my head, and I said to myself, *What was that?* I knew whatever it was . . . it wasn't good. I exited the stall and went to look in the mirror, but I couldn't see anything. I backed up to the door and took one more look, and that's where they found me. Someone rushed out to the audience and asked, "Is someone here with Marla Gibbs?" My sister Frieda spoke up, and they told her they found me on the floor by the door in the bathroom.

It was 2006. I was rushed to a hospital nearby the theater, where they discovered I had a brain aneurysm. The doctors told my family that I had two days maximum to have brain surgery, and if not, I would die from the damage. They further explained how dangerous the surgery was and that if I was lucky enough to survive, there was a high probability that I would never act or possibly even walk again. Their exact words were "Your mother's life as you know it is over." They suggested that we start getting my will in order. They told my family that they were the best at doing this kind of surgery. My daughter later told me that she hadn't bought that they were the right doctors for the job. She said her Spirit told her that the doctors would benefit more from being able to say they performed the surgery on Marla Gibbs, but it was not going to benefit me. In fact, the rest of my family wasn't buying it or their diagnosis of "no hope" either, and told them in regards to my career being over, "You don't know our mother!" Everyone had been there all night, so when morning came, Angela, Frieda, and my grandson Amil left. Angela felt she needed to shower and reset so she could do some research while my youngest son, Dorian, took the first shift and sat by my side. On the way home, Angela called her longtime friend Diane Stephenson and asked her to place me on her group's prayer list.

"What are we praying for?" she asked. Angela asked her to keep it confidential and told her what happened.

Diane asked the question that we all believed helped to save my life: "Do you know Dr. Keith Black at Cedars?" A few hours later, Angela was on the phone with Dr. Black, chair of the neurological department at Cedars-Sinai Hospital. Angela called Dorian, who was still by my side, and he told me that Dr. Black was going to have me transferred to Cedars, and I agreed. I was in and out of consciousness at that point. Interestingly enough, when Angela told the doctors at the hospital she was moving me to Cedars, they suddenly felt it was a great idea.

Cedars was definitely the right move. Dr. Black assigned

world-renowned surgeon Dr. Wouter Schievink to perform the operation because of his success with aneurysms, and that's why I'm here today to tell this story. But it wasn't easy. First of all, they had to perform two surgeries, because after the first one, I wasn't responding. I had a stroke right after the first surgery. My daughter tells me that she came into the room and asked me to fight before the second surgery. She had been strong up to that point but was starting to worry. She said I whispered, "I will," and squeezed her hand. It gave her the strength to keep believing I would make it. Two of my stepdaughters, Gisele and Yolanda, flew in immediately and were there during the surgery and part of my recovery. My sister Frieda was there too. Everyone held each other up and took shifts being by my side. They wanted me to know that every time I opened my eyes, someone was there who loved me. It's so important to have your family advocate for you in the hospital. My grandson was living in St. Louis but flew in and stayed throughout my recovery. My son Jordan took the late-night shift, my son Dorian took the early-morning shift, and my grandson and daughter took shifts during the day. My family did research on aneurysms and asked important questions. I know I really made it back because my family's care was vigilant. I'm thankful for them and blessed. The second surgery was successful, and then the real work began. I had to learn how to walk, talk, and do little things like pick up a spoon or chew my food.

The brain is like a computer and is really amazing. My grandson Amil told me that when I was in the ICU, he was sitting by my bedside, and I waved him over to come closer. When he leaned in, I asked him, "What's eight times seven?"

He told me, "Fifty-six," and then I kept going: Eight times eight equals sixty-four, eight times nine equals seventy-two, etc. He was so excited and told the family "G'ma is in there doing times tables!" Of course, I don't remember any of this. In fact, I don't remember being in the hospital at all.

When my humor came back, my family said they knew I was going to be all right. The nurse told them I was kicking the covers off, and she said, "Ms. Gibbs, you don't want nobody to see up your gown."

I replied, "Who's looking?"

My daughter said that after the surgery I asked her, "Did you see that fine Dr. Black?" My daughter also told me I was mad at the nurse because she let the doctor take the phone from me.

When Angela asked the nurse what happened, the nurse told her, "Your mother was ordering stuff from HSN [the Home Shopping Network], and the doctor walked in as she was giving them her credit card number," which I had obviously memorized. My family still has a good time with that, so, yes, I'll admit, I order shit all the time. I guess even when I'm not in my right mind.

Another story they love teasing me about is, when some of my friends wanted to see me, the family would always ask, "Do you want so-and-so to come?" I would shake my head yes or no, and of course they would honor that. I was still in the ICU with tubes everywhere, so I really didn't want company.

One day my son Dorian asked, "Is there anyone you really want to see?"

To which I replied, "Call Billy Dee!" My brain was coming back bit by bit, but it was a long road to recovery.

In rehab is when I really started allowing visitors. Dick Anthony Williams, my close friend, would come and sit with me. Alaina Reed Hall came every day and brought me juice. My girl Jeanne King was there all the time and said, "Please don't forget I was here," and I didn't. My spiritual granddaughter Gina Loring (my friend William Marshall's daughter) came and read me poetry, brought me juice, and also came to the house and cooked. Doreet, the raw food chef, would bring me fresh juices and raw meals. Ben Vereen would come and bring his dog for me to play with. Ben had a stroke while walking in Malibu and was then hit by a car, so he knew firsthand what the road to recovery was going to be, and he was there for me. The director from the MOA Wellness Center, Ron, came and performed their purifying energy healing on me a few times, and my daughter's close friend Mahasin, who is another energy healer, also brought her crystals and worked her magic. Angela's friend Shay came and helped braid my hair once they took the bandages off. My daughter said I was not allowed many visitors because my brain was mending itself and could not take a lot of stimulation. Even watching television was too much in the early stages. For that reason, a lot of friends couldn't come see me. I needed that time to heal. But I really appreciated how much love and concern my friends and extended family showed me and my family. Rosie Lee Hooks brought food and water for Angela, and Adleane Hunter would bring her Starbucks and sit with her. All of it mattered, and all of it helped me recover, and for that I am forever grateful.

Most people do not survive brain aneurysms, so I knew God still had plans for me. The more my strength and memory came back, the more trouble I got into. I'm a Gemini, and my mind is always curious and always working . . . not always for the better. For instance, I did not want to use diapers while in rehab. I wanted to go to the bathroom on my own. The bathroom was right next to my bed, so I could not understand why I needed help to get there. Every time I was alone in the room, I would sneak out of the bed and end up on the floor. My family finally had to ask them to tie me to the bed. I watched carefully as the nurses tied me up so I could untie myself as soon as they left. And you guessed it . . . I'd be on the floor again. I said to myself, *Marla, we gotta stop ending up down here. We're not getting anywhere.*

There was just something inside me that kept saying, *It ain't over.* But when I got home and looked at the old woman staring back at me in the mirror, I said, "Maybe it is over." Maybe my days as an actress were gone.

Recovery was hard, and it took every ounce of physical, mental, and spiritual strength I could muster. I started questioning why it had happened, especially when I still had so many plans for my life. I was getting ready to tour with my new jazz CD, but as they say, man makes plans and God laughs. This wasn't funny, though. I sank into a deep depression. I felt like maybe it was time for me to go. I didn't want to get up. I didn't want to do anything.

My family had a caretaker come and help. She would fix breakfast and help clean, but it was just a difficult time. It's humbling when you can't do anything for yourself. My mind told me I could walk, but I couldn't without help. I went to outpatient rehab for occupational, physical, and speech therapy. As I progressed, they had me do a light jog across the room. My friend Chrystal Carmichael from Detroit came to help. The first day she got here, we went walking, and then I wanted to show her I could jog, and I fell and hit my head. It was embarrassing, but mostly it was disheartening. I complained to the rehab center, and the nurse said, "We didn't tell you to jog at home!" I finally accepted where I was at in my recovery. I had always been an independent woman who juggled multiple projects. Now I was totally dependent and could do nothing. Acceptance of where I was in my recovery was essential to me healing, and I think acceptance is the key to healing in life.

Earlier that year, in June 2006, I was finally brave enough to fully embrace my dream of singing. My good friend H. B. Barnum, a pianist, arranger, and record producer, had called out of the blue and asked if I'd do an album. He had previously asked me to perform for the Marines in San Diego. I had been so nervous. I'd stood in the wings before it was my time to step onstage and said, "Okay, Billie [I was talking to Billie Holliday], we do this all the time, so it's no big thing." I psyched myself up, and the performance went very well. So well, that H.B. was convinced it was time for me to do an album. He said it would only cost about ten thousand dollars to record. Forty thousand dollars later, *Never Too Late* was completed.

When I started working on the album, I thought I'd be working with the musicians live, but the instrumentation was done before I got there, and wow, it sounded so good that I was even more inspired. I grew up listening to jazz greats like Sarah Vaughan, Billie Holliday, Billy Eckstine, and Dinah Washington. The CD is really my contribution to a genre I love and a tribute to some of the artists who did it best.

We had a listening party for the album at the Wilshire Ebell Theatre, and so many of my friends showed up. My girls Beverly Todd and Judy Pace were there. Shirley and

Bernard Kinsey, Nichelle Nichols, Ja'Net DuBois, my sister Frieda, my then-accountant Errol Collier, and the list goes on. It was a dream come true for me to have so many people that I admired supporting my music. H.B. and I started talking about putting a tour together. I was getting excited about going over to Europe and performing in some of the jazz clubs there, but God had other plans. That was when I had the aneurysm, and my dreams and reality crashed into each other. No tours, no singing in clubs—in fact, no singing at all. It hurt. Acceptance of and surrender to the present can sometimes devastate you. But there is always something to learn, an opportunity for expansion.

We didn't let anyone know I had an aneurysm, so most people don't know about it to this day. We didn't want the industry to find out because we thought it would hurt my chances to work again. Angela made sure nobody knew. BET called the hospital, as did a couple news outlets, but I was under another name. My family really took good care of me and protected me, and my friends made sure I knew how much I was loved—for that I will always be grateful.

As I was recovering from the aneurysm, I was told that the years of eating well, as well as taking herbs and supplements, played a major role in my healing. That made me really happy. After two years of rehabilitation, I was feeling up to full speed again. I was working out with a trainer and had a daily routine of walking with my neighbor Betty. One day

I was rushing to meet Betty and grabbed an outfit that I not only didn't like but hadn't worn in quite a while. I was standing on my right leg while trying to jam my left foot into the leg of the pants. My leg went down into the pants and back. The momentum knocked me backward, and I landed on my foot. My foot folded in half, and I heard a big crack. At first it didn't hurt because I was in shock, but once the pain came, it was unbearable. I called 911, and they suggested I go to the hospital.

My son Joey took me, and after the exam they told me, "You really know how to break your foot. You have split your metatarsal and fractured three toes."

I had to have foot surgery, and unbeknownst to me, the doctor fused two tendons together. Vanessa Bell Calloway's husband, Dr. Tony Calloway, was my anesthesiologist. It was New Year's Eve when I had the operation, and Tony saw my daughter at their New Year's Eve party. Tony warned her that "your mom is going to be in a lot of pain when she wakes up. Let me know if she needs anything." He was right, and I was grateful for the warning and the help.

I have pins and two screws in my foot. I've been waiting for my toes to heal ever since, and they haven't. My daughter took me to see Dr. Noreen Oswell at Cedars-Sinai's Foot Center not long after the surgery. Dr. Oswell was not only easy to talk to, but she was also extremely knowledgeable and explained to me what the surgeon had done and that unfortunately she was not able to return the use of my toes. Dr. Oswell discussed shoe options, and I left hopeful, although it was clear that my high-heel days were over for sure!

Once again my recovery was hard and long. I kept wondering, *What is happening to me? Why am I having these challenges? What do I need to learn?* In retrospect, it was probably because I kept doing stupid things. There's nothing like a health emergency to give new meaning to the phrase "It's never too late." My crisis was an aneurysm. I survived it and felt like I was given another chance to move forward doing the things I love to do for a living and with the people I admire. This is the greatest of blessings—after seeing my children thrive.

CHAPTER TEN

Faith Is the Final Word

We cannot sit and wait for a miracle
to come knocking on our door.
We are the miracle.

In the book *The Power of Now*, author Eckhart Tolle explains that the only place we have power is in the present moment . . . the here and NOW. I finally had to realize it was time for me to stop the race to recovery and to pace myself, because healing was going to be a marathon. It was time to be still. It was time to surrender to the NOW and to God. This took faith, tenacity, and patience.

I decided that if I was going to be thirty, I figured I ought to act like it. I gave myself a pep talk and stopped looking in the mirror. Instead I began looking within, because I knew that was where God was. I soon started exercising more consistently, and after about six months, I learned to walk again.

I believe it's important to be a participant in your own healing. I also believe that we benefit from looking beyond Western medicine and doctors' opinions as a way to maintain our health. Doctors practice medicine—the operative word being "practice." And while I have a healthy respect for this profession—and in my case, it saved my life—I also respect Eastern medicine and holistic healing, and I wish the two worlds would merge. Health insurance companies will not cover alternative medicine, so many people can't afford it.

Western medicine practitioners would often frown when I told them about my regime of herbs and supplements. They never asked me what I ate and were quick to prescribe medication. This was disappointing. I valued Eastern medicine and its philosophies, which include nutrition, diet, and mindset. Maybe that's why I was so stubborn about taking blood pressure medication. I wanted a plan. A plan to find the source of my high blood pressure and not just treat the symptom. You'd think all the smoking I'd done would have been the cause of my aneurysm, but mine had to do with blood pressure. I discovered I had high blood pressure as far back as when I was working at United Airlines in Detroit. One of my coworkers knew I was having bad headaches that started in the back of my head. She told me her husband was concerned and suggested I go see a doctor, and that's how I found out I had it. The doctor put me on blood pressure medicine, which I took, but my blood pressure remained a problem. Of course, back then no one was talking about diet, and it didn't help that I kept trying to juggle working during the day, running the numbers at night, raising three kids, and surviving my abusive marriage.

I was also hyperactive and loved having five things to do at one time. If I could get them all done, it would make me very happy. The headaches eventually stopped, so I discontinued taking the medicine, because it never worked and I didn't like taking medication. I was always trying to get the doctor to take me off of it. I would get this feeling that was like an adrenaline rush in my head, but I didn't recognize it as high blood pressure. I recognized it as motivation. This, of course, eventually would prove to be a problem.

My former husband and the father of my children, Buddy Gibbs, transitioned in 1998, having lived with colon cancer for close to six months. Having served in the Marines, he chose a veterans' hospital for his treatment. I encouraged him to try alternative medical approaches too. But he wasn't open to that, believing that he'd made the right choice.

Buddy called me in a panic from the hospital, pleading for me to come get him. I spoke to his doctor, who explained to me what was happening. Buddy was in terrible pain. Hooked up to machines, he was not in a position to go anywhere. I think what the doctor was saying to him was that his end was nearing. He quieted down and got off the phone.

The next time I went to visit Buddy, we had a difficult

but necessary talk. "We've all decided to be cremated," I said to him. "But I do have one plot left if you want to be buried and have a funeral, or do you want to be cremated?" He said he wanted to be cremated.

We had a service on a boat in the ocean, where we scattered his ashes. We put his ashes in a basket with rose petals on the top, so when they lowered the ashes, the petals stayed on the water's surface, so you knew where they were. We circled the spot three times, and during that time, in my Spirit, I heard him say, "Thank you."

Buddy was more than the bad behavior he exhibited toward me and the children, and I bore him no bitterness in his last days, nor after he was gone. He was a US Marine who received the Purple Heart twice. He studied and became an accountant, and while in Detroit he worked for the Army Corp of Engineers. In Los Angeles he joined the Post, the city's branch of the Society of American Military Engineers, loved it, and received more awards. In later years he tried to reconnect with his kids, and before he died, we all became friendly. The Post gave him a twenty-one-gun salute.

We have to go within ourselves to find the solutions and responses to our problems and obstacles, especially in times when we don't feel seen and supported. That's where we find God, our greatest source of support. Every time I took one step toward my goals, dreams, and blessings, God took two big other steps for me. I adjusted my attitude to be more positive. I began to truly believe that abundance was mine for the asking. That's how I overcame many defeats. I moved with faith and spoke what I wanted into existence.

There were the life skills I learned by way of acting, which helped me turn my life around, and then there was my personal spiritual development. Watching television one day, I was introduced to Science of Mind. It was right after Angela had hit Buddy over the head with the bottle and we had to flee. We were staying in a back room of my aunt's house, and the program came on. It was my answer, the light at a time of darkness. When I joined the Science of Mind church, I learned about the spiritual laws, especially the power of forgiveness and compassion. I had to forgive my mother for leaving me, for example. I had to find compassion for who she had been at sixteen when she first got pregnant and was put out of the home. Her mother had died when she was four years old. She'd felt abandoned by the parent who'd passed away and the living adults who'd turned away from her. She hadn't known how to be a good mother to me because she hadn't known what that looked like. She hadn't been taught how to be a mother. I learned that what often blocked us from reaching our dreams is the energy we put into holding on to our stories. Forgiveness is so important to freeing up the energy we need to move forward. The path to success—no matter how you define it—does not follow a straight line.

So many actors I came up with thought they had the

passion for acting but didn't. They'd tell me, "I'm giving this six months, and if it doesn't happen by then, I'm out." That mentality means either you're not really passionate about it, or you don't have the understanding to know that these things don't happen in your time but in God's time. Ego makes us compare ourselves to others and pressures us to gain material goals on a time clock that we create. Comparisons are an enemy to patience and faith. The Universe has Divine wisdom, and if we trust and keep our channel open, our time will come, and it will be better than we expected.

Artists do what we do because we love it. We do it because we have to.

What really drove me was a passion to get out of myself and my reality. Becoming other characters allowed me to live their lives. I could make the transition into women who were rich, successful, loved, powerful, or whatever the role called for. That was my motivation.

Each of us is challenged to find the things and people in life who motivate us to persevere.

Acting was easier for me than singing. With singing I feel like you're asking people to accept you. My confidence wasn't at that level where I could expose myself. But with acting I was asking people to accept the character, so if they didn't like the character, that was okay, because that was separate from me. The other reward from acting is that I get to go on the journey of the character and therefore broaden my perspective on life and gain a deeper connection with people because I've shared their experiences . . . at least to some degree.

I believe that when God puts us on this earth, we are given a good dose of self-confidence to make it through life. Trouble is that family, environment, and social constructs also have impacts on our confidence and sense of self, making it easy for us to drift away from who we truly are. Once we lose our connection to self, it is hard to find our way back, especially because we look outside of ourselves for approval and validation.

Best way I know to get it back in step is to go inside again. And put our faith in ourselves and in God. It can be scary at first. It's my positive attitude that's kept me from being defeated by life's everyday occurrences.

You have to keep moving forward with faith while speaking what you want into existence. Into the Universe. I learned that the Universe conspires to bring you the desires of your heart when you believe. Truly believe. I'd look at the TV and say, "I want to do that show. Thank you." I was already thanking the Universe for the shows, and sure enough, *Cold Case* and *ER* and others called and offered me roles.

After the *227* series ended, I did a number of recurring and guest-starring roles on various hit shows. I started booking again after my recovery. I got to play with my TV daughter, Regina King, again on the show *Southland*. A funny story: The director told me to surprise Regina when she came to my door and to call her Brenda, her character's name from *227*, so I did. Regina is such a consummate professional, she never broke character, although her eyes did widen for a second, but she kept right on going. It is such a rich and funny moment between us. I love any opportunity I get to work with her.

I am blessed to continuously work, because that's what you do when you're thirty. Truth is, I don't know what to do with myself when I'm not working. Exploring different characters still continues to intrigue me. When people tell me how they look forward to retiring, I always say, "I don't want to retire from nothing!"

Hot in Cleveland brought me together with Betty White, who was another actor who showed no signs of retiring. An avid animal lover like me, Betty said she had to keep working to support her animal causes. I am so glad I got to work with Robert Forster on the *Breaking Bad* movie, *El Camino*, before he made his transition. What a gentleman. I also got to team up with Sherman Hemsley again in *Tyler Perry's House of Payne*, and then I worked with Tyler again in his *Madea's Witness Protection* movie. Tyler was so good to me, and I am so proud of what he has done for the industry. I've always said we need our own network and studios, and Tyler did that! I love the African proverb "Until the lion learns how to write, every story will glorify the hunter." Because of Tyler

Perry, Oprah Winfrey, Ava DuVernay, Shonda Rhimes, and Kenya Barris, I'm happy to say there are more of us owning our stories. Now the lion has become the storyteller.

As far as the performing arts goes, I feel I have reached success, because I've worked consistently. In my personal life, I don't feel the major success, because when I'm not working, I don't feel the same connection. If I wake up but don't have anything to do or I'm not contributing to someone's life, I start to wonder why I am still here.

Somehow Spirit responds to me and starts sending work. I put into the Universe what I want the Universe to respond to. My thing is, I want to work, so I'm going to take Christ at His word. I mean for everything, honey. For example, if I'm driving along and I want to move over into the next lane, I say, "I want to go in that lane," and in a minute or so, somebody will slow up, allowing me room to move over. I say thank you, and I get in the lane. I expect it to happen, so it happens. If by chance, the opposite happens, I know that's the day I didn't say thank you or ask for what I wanted. Or I need to be reminded to be patient and go with the flow. I think it's really that simple. Life isn't always easy, but it is simpler than we make it. You have to really "accept the things you cannot change and change the things you can and have the wisdom to know the difference," just as the Serenity Prayer states. When I started operating my life from this principle, my life started opening up in wonderful ways.

It took me years to get to this mindset. But being part of a spiritual community helped. I see now that the Almighty had a plan for my life, because even when I moved to Los Angeles, it was laid out for me. That's when I realized I was supposed to be in California. Given that, I can't be mad or dwell on what happened to me, because it was all just a means to an end.

I mentioned working with D. L. Hughley, and how much fun that was!

Being on *Martin* was a hoot! I played Minnie, the housekeeper from hell, and had a ball! Martin Lawrence is truly an OG in the business. He, Tichina Arnold, and Tisha Campbell treated me like royalty. I had a great time giving them a hard time. When Tisha had her club Zen, I went to see her perform, and she pulled me on the stage with her. Both Tisha and Tichina can sing . . . Wait, let me say that another way . . . Both of them girls can SANG, chile!

I had the opportunity to play a lesbian in two different shows. The first one was *Cold Case*. The second time was in *Scandal*, when I played the lifelong partner of Olivia Pope's neighbor, who I eventually learned was killed. Kerry Washington's character, Olivia, had been kidnapped, and her team couldn't figure out how or by whom until I came in, asking, "Where is the Black lady?"

It was a two-part character arc for me, and when I came back for the second episode, Kerry stopped and said, "Everybody, this is royalty." I get a mixture of feelings whenever I hear this. I am certainly warmed by it. I also feel appreciated for the time I've put into this business. I'm just so grateful that all these years I've gotten to make a living doing what I love, and being acknowledged for it is the icing on the cake. I wouldn't feel right moving on from this role without acknowledging how difficult and yet how brave the nonbinary population is for bringing the conversation around gender bias to the forefront. I played a role that I discarded after I left the set. But you cannot or should not feel you have to discard or discount who you truly are. We are all one—I say that all the time. We are all from the same race . . . the human race, and we all deserve our human rights to be respected and protected.

I have to mention that crazy genius Dave Chappelle. When my agents told me that I was being asked to do his show, my daughter was a big fan and encouraged me to do it. I read the script, and when I met Dave, I said, "You know you're out of your mind, right?"

Dave answered, "So they tell me."

I had so much fun on the set, and Dave's team treated my Amil and me really well. Charles Barkley was on the same episode, and we got to hang and laugh with him as well. I am proud to be a part of Dave's iconic *Chappelle's Show*, which is now part of pop culture history. Congratulations to Dave. I'm so encouraged by his decision to leave the show and put his integrity before money. I respect Dave for that. A person should not compromise their personal beliefs and their creative gifts because they are afraid that they'll lose their seat at the table.

He received so much criticism for leaving and going to Africa. Then, a decade later, he was blessed with the Netflix deal and received exponentially more millions than what he walked away from! Now he can build his own table! God always gets the last and best laugh.

Today I'm so proud of the many talented people of color who are now showrunners, writers, and creators, and I'm happy they think of me. Shonda Rhimes is one of them with *Scandal*. I did two episodes, and working with the cast was absolutely great. The bonus was in the second episode—all my scenes were with Kerry Washington, who was wonderful to work with.

Jerrod Carmichael is another creative writer I had a ball working with. Jerrod's *The Carmichael Show* was funny, irreverent, and poignant. David Alan Grier played the role of Joe Carmichael. I played Francis, his mother and grandmother to Jerrod and Bobby. Francis, stricken with dementia, wanted her son Joe to help her die. Francis wanted her life to end before she lost all her memories. Of course, Joe refuses, which leaves Jerrod and Bobby, played by Lil Rel Howery, to try to talk Francis out of her decision. The character Francis also had a penchant for comparing their skin color to chocolate bars that kept getting darker and darker.

Jerrod knows how to take serious issues and find humorous ways to explore them. Also starring in the show was Loretta Devine as Cynthia, the mother. I so admire Loretta, who has the title of the hardest-working Black actor in Hollywood.

In *Black-ish*, created by showrunner Kenya Barris, I got to work with my friend Jenifer Lewis, who is as funny as she is talented. I played Mabel Johnson, the mother of Earl "Pops" Johnson, played by Laurence Fishburne. Beau Bridges played Tracee Ellis Ross's father. I was proud of the scene they wrote for me, in which I talk about Black women serving their men. I told them that when I came up, Black men were degraded at every turn, but at home, we women—as wives, sisters, and mothers—did our best to give them their dignity back. It was important to me, because it was true.

One of the roles that will always remain the most memorable is when I was asked to reprise my character of Florence on *Live in Front of a Studio Audience: Norman Lear's "All in the Family" and "The Jeffersons."* As I mentioned, I've been told that Jamie Foxx and Jackée Harry approached Norman Lear individually and asked for me to play Florence. I was forty-four years old when I landed that role in 1975, and then forty-four years later, I walked onto the set to do it again and remembered all my lines. Everything came back to me, even the blocking. The audience was waiting to see who they cast for Florence, and when I walked through the door, the audience lost it for so long, we had to hold. Jamie told me that the moment was overwhelming, and he had to fight to hold it together. I've always been a fan of his, and now I'm happy to consider him a dear friend. Thank you to Norman Lear and Jimmy Kimmel for coming up with the idea of the reboot.

Sometimes I have to ask myself, *Are you still thirty?* Seriously, after all this time, I still have to remind myself that it's never too late. I've learned that life is not a destination; we never get "there." We are always on the journey of the unknown, and that's what keeps us young and curious. When I ask myself, *Are you still thirty?*, of course the answer is yes, so next I say, *Then get up and get busy!*

The Universe hears me, because things start moving in a positive direction. My grandson Amil has always loved the jazz album I did in 2006. Actually, Amil composed two songs on it. It was his idea to remaster the CD and re-release it. Amil was working for Brandhorse Creative agency, where they were able to see search engine results from tons of people who were asking, "Is Marla Gibbs still alive?" And "What happened to Marla Gibbs?" This struck a nerve in Amil. He had witnessed my long journey to recovery, a significant lull in my career, and we had discussed my feelings, where I had shared, "I think it's over. Maybe it's my time to go." Amil had the insight to rebrand me and bring me into the digital era. He built a presence on social media that reconnected me not only with fans but also with my colleagues, who would reach out to let me know how I'd inspired them, and that resulted in new bookings on shows. With this new online community and social media buzz, my agents had fuel to start what would be the next phase of my career. Needless to say, this buzz got me motivated, and it gave me a new sense of purpose and presence. When you change your mind, you can change your life. The downward spiral I had been experiencing after the aneurysm was over. I realized that, during the holding pattern, God had gotten my attention. It is always darkest before dawn, and a new dawn is always on the horizon.

I've also learned that forgiveness is the key to joy, freedom, and personal peace. When you forgive people, you also free yourself from your story. We sometimes hold on to our hurtful stories as parts of our identities. We often think forgiving someone means that we have to be okay with what that person did to us. Nothing could be further from the truth. Forgiveness is about understanding the lessons we learned from those events and how they serve us now. It also releases any power that person or experience once had over you. To forgive is to release. I've learned that for-giving is forth-giving . . . It means to give forth the love, tolerance, and compassion you want someone to give to you. The trick is that you have to be forth-giving to you first. Forth-giving of empathy, patience, and love to yourself. This is real freedom. This is real peace. After I forgave myself for mistakes I had made, it was easier to work on forgiving my Grandmother Hattie and Aunt Bell for all their abuse. I realized that I was carrying a weight by not forgiving them. I also had to forgive my mother for leaving me. I began to understand what she was going through when I became an adult.

People ask me about being in an abusive marriage, and that doesn't even sound right for me to say anymore, because I understand what my ex-husband was going through and where he was in his head at that point. Now I understand even better. That experience was a tool in the hand of God. Before my ex-husband passed, I said to him, "Listen, there's probably some stuff I did that you didn't like that contributed to the breakup, so I just want to apologize for anything I did because I was an insecure person."

He replied, "Don't you understand I was very insecure too?" I was shocked when he said this because he'd carried himself with an air of superiority, so I would never have thought of him as being insecure. I'd always thought I was less than him. But now I realize that bullies are insecure, which is why they behave that way. In retrospect, I now understand that everything that happened to me was ordained. If my husband had been loving, I would have stayed in Detroit. Getting away from him and the abuse led to my escape to Los Angeles, where I was able to live out my destiny.

The greatest lesson I've learned is, you have to forgive people because they're doing exactly what they're supposed to do. In Caroline Myss's book *Sacred Contracts*, she talks about "the key relationships we have with people who are here to help us learn the lessons we have agreed to work on."

These individual contracts are part of the sacred contracts, as written with the Divine. My lesson was to learn I had a personal connection with the Source and that this Presence was within me all along. I had to learn my worth, though, in order to embrace this and to trust it. I've discovered that to forgive is just as important as it is to love.

I truly believe everything we do and everyone we meet are put in our path for a purpose. There are no accidents; we're all teachers and students. I do believe that, though this statement may be overused, it is true, and that is, if you can conceive something and if you truly believe it, you can achieve it. Some people say, "I'll believe it when I see it," but the truth is . . . you'll see it when you believe it! It's called faith! Faith, just like love . . . is a verb. Put them in action! And love for self is the most important, because without it, we're always seeking love from the outside. That is dangerous and unsustainable. Sometimes our traumas get in the way of being able to unpeel the layers that harm us. I had to learn to let go of the need to control and to be willing to finally seek counsel. And if you are listening and trusting your inner compass, you will know when it's time to seek and when it's time to be still. We also have to pay attention to the lessons we learn, trust our intuition, and not be afraid to take risks. We must learn when to say yes to life and no to toxic people or situations. We want to remember that we create our reality. We cannot sit and wait for a miracle to come knocking on our door. We are the miracle.

I've learned not to worry about age and simply think about what I want to do with my life and know that I can still do it. No matter what age I am, if I want to accomplish something, I'm going to give it a try.

I have finally stopped worrying about what I'm going to do next, because it's not important. We have today. Today is the present. And if we truly have faith, then we know that as long as we are breathing . . . it's never too late.

I had an inspiration for a song on my jazz album titled "It's Never Too Late."

The lyrics say:

As long as you breathe
You'd better believe
It's never too late for life
Drop all that fear
'Cus as long as you're here
It's never too late for life
Scheme your schemes
Dream your dreams

Living your life is the way
You cannot borrow from tomorrow
You only get one day
So don't give me the blues
'Cus I've got good news
It's never too late for life
Start being bold and stick to your goals
Forget all that stress and strive
Just keep the faith and trust your heart
Use your head now, that being said
It's never, never too late for life
It's never too late for life

I hope these pages have given you a peek into my world as I moved from Margaret to Marla and what I survived or overcame to reach my dreams. I hope I made you smile and perhaps pause and contemplate your own story, the one you are writing and living every day. I pray my life and the lessons learned will inspire you to be what God intended for you. May you live your best life without the need for permission or apology, because if you do, you will give those around you permission to do the same. The world is waiting for your unique gifts, and if you let doubt, or age, or your past stop you, we will not ever have them. It's never too late, honey . . . keep living and keep loving.

God bless you, and thank you for all the years of joy and love you have given me.

Acknowledgments

First let me say—this kind of thing is always tricky, because when you've lived as long and loved as wide as I have, honey, the list is long. So, if your name ain't here, but your love was felt, know that you are still in my heart and part of my story.

To my children—Angela, Dorian, and Jordan—thank you for walking every step of this life with me. You each taught me something different about love, strength, and showing up. Angela, your vision, your voice, and your commitment made this book happen. You held the mirror and said, "Mama, it's time." And Amil, my brilliant grandson—you didn't just keep me current on social media, baby; you carried this legacy into the future, had it written in stone, and helped turn our family story into a movement. I'm proud of you beyond words.

To all my nieces, nephews, and extended family: Thank you for holding me up when I needed it, for rooting for me,